OLD WAYS OF WORKING WOOD

Old Ways of Working Wood

By Alex W. Bealer

BARRE PUBLISHERS
Barre, Massachusetts
1972

TO MY DEAR HELEN.

who has demonstrated singular patience over the years in waiting for me to make things out of wood.

Contents

Introduction

MAN has an affinity with wood.

For a million years or more mankind has used wood to supplement his hands and to extend his authority, his comforts and his range. Certain anthropologists now theorize that mankind is directly descended from a club-carrying ape, and surely the club was of wood. Primitive man has always used wood extensively for weapons, tools, houses, transportation, utensils and a host of other uses. Modern civilized man uses it for the same purposes, but in greater quantities, the main difference being in the methods of shaping and adapting it to modern uses. In the twentieth century, power tools have taken the place of hand tools and science has to some extent replaced talent, but the affinity between man and wood has remained.

Indeed, the demand for timber has had great historical significance on more than one occasion. Lief Ericson discovered America five hundred years before Columbus because he sought a ready supply of essential timber for the Norse settlements in treeless Greenland. Had it not been for the vast oak forests of Britain, which lasted until Tudor times, England might never have ruled the waves for there would have been no material with which to build her fleets. When Jamestown, the initial colony of the subsequent British empire, was founded it was sustained to a great extent during its first year by shipping clapboards riven by hand from the oaks growing in the seemingly endless forests of the New World.

Wood, of course, is a marvelous medium for craftsmanship because it offers such a variety of natural characteristics for specialized uses. Some species of trees are soft, others almost as hard as iron. Some split easily, others defy splitting. Some types of wood are elastic, others brittle. Man, over the ages, has adapted the various woods each to its most appropriate use, and he has developed tools and techniques with which to exploit the nature of different trees. By developing a host of ingenious hand tools, he has made wood serve him since the beginning of time.

One of the best descriptions of why and how wood was adapted to special uses in the pre-industrial age is the poem, "The Deacon's Masterpiece, or The Wonderful 'One Hoss Shay,'" by Oliver Wendell Holmes. One remembers that the marvelous equipage described in the poem was designed "to last a hundred years and a day," thereby becoming a paean to the durability of wood used properly as well as to the variety of its uses. We quote:

> . . . So the Deacon inquired of the village folk
> Where he could find the strongest oak,
> That couldn't be split nor bent nor broke,—
> That was for spokes and floor and sills;
> He sent for lancewood to make the thills;
> The crossbars were ash, from the straightest trees,
> The panels of whitewood, that cuts like cheese,
> But lasts like iron for things like these;
> The hubs of logs from the "Settler's ellum,"—
> Last of its timber—they couldn't sell 'em,
> Never an axe had seen their chips,
> And the wedges flew from between their lips,
> Their blunt ends frizzled like celery-tips; . . .

What Holmes did not describe in his poem were the tools used to shape the various parts of the shay. Carriage makers in particular used a multiplicity of tools in shaping axles, hubs, spokes and felloes for the wheels. For the finer work on the body each carriage maker had an extensive set of planes, some large, some tiny, many of them wee things of beauty that fit into the palm of the hand. Each of these jewels was designed to do perfectly some special job which gave the carriage its shape and grace and strength and lightness. Coffin makers used many of the same tools.

Carriage makers and coffin makers, however, were only two of a number of woodworking trades, each of which used its own specialized woodworking tools as well as sharing a few basic tools with all other woodworkers. These other masters in shaping and joining wood included carpenters, cabinetmakers, wheelwrights and wainwrights ("wright" meaning "worker," "wrought" meaning "worked"), board makers, housewrights, millwrights, instrument makers, coopers, joiners, turners and a few related trades such as woodcutters, sawyers and gun-stockers.

In olden times, roughly from the Middle Ages until around 1840 in America and 1900 or later in Europe, the artisan was more important than his tools. He was, of course, dependent on the special tools of his trade, but he used his tools to shape wood as he desired rather than design his work to fit the limitations of his machines as is common in modern industry. Also, the old time artisan had no compunction about designing new tools to do special jobs. Each of his tools was but an extension of himself. His individuality became immortal in his work.

All that has changed at an accelerating pace since machinery and mass production were developed and since the convenience and ubiquity of electric and pneumatic power have appeared. Modern technology, with its vast capacity to produce cheaply everything needed by a burgeoning world population, has replaced the hand tools and the hand craftsmen which have attended mankind since its earliest days. The gentle rhythm of the hand-saw has almost disappeared on construction sites and in the shops of cabinet workers. It has been displaced by the shrill, angry whine of the power saw, not necessarily for any lack of esthetic feeling on the part of modern contractors but because one man with a power saw can do the work of ten men with only a hand-saw apiece.

For a long time now great mills, noisy with huge machines and noxious with fumes and sawdust, have been the sole suppliers to house builders for limited patterns of framing mold for doors and windows, crown and baseboard molds for trimming the rooms of modern houses.

How different this is from the housebuilding of the eighteenth and early nineteenth centuries. Then the contractor proudly bore the title of master carpenter. His molding of all sorts was carved from carefully selected strips of white pine, or chestnut or walnut, with a set of hand molding planes, some of which he had made himself to his own design. When his houses were built each room had an individuality, a warmth, a reflection of personality impossible to find in the prefabricated units which attempt to house the results of the population explosion, or even in the architect-supervised, expensive mansions of the affluent.

Of course, the reasons for this degeneration of the artisan are both social and economic. There could never be found today an adequate number of master carpenters conversant with hand tools to build a fraction of the houses needed in the last half of the twentieth century. Also, if enough carpenters were found they could never build houses quickly enough to keep up with the demand and, in addition, only the richest could afford such houses. Volume and quick profit are the essential requirements of modern building. The same requirements must be met in furniture making and other facets of the woodworking industry.

As a consequence, the machine, not the craftsman, dominates woodworking today. In common carpentry the introduction of the power saw, among the first of the hand power tools, has been followed by eagerly accepted power drills and power planes. Indeed, power hammers are now commonplace in certain fields of woodworking including the manufacture of prefabricated houses, and much furniture is made with the convenience and speed provided by that stepchild of the hammer, the stapling machine. By the twenty-first century hammers, descendants of man's earliest tool, the *coup de poing* [blow with the fist], might disappear almost entirely as new amazing adhesives are developed which can actually weld wood together through chemical bonding.

This rapid evolution of woodworking from artistic craft to productive science has happened in only a few years, a couple of generations. The result has been artistic tragedy to a degree. The old hand tools, familiar to our grandfathers, tools similar in form to those found in the shop of Joseph of Nazareth, have suddenly become so rare and unfamiliar in their variety and beauty that the shape and function of many are no longer recognized and few are appreciated. The ingenuity of principle reflected by each of them, the genius of design formulated when the man animal decided to be civilized, are generally lost on modern man.

There is further loss in the universal adoption of power tools. Consider the lost emotional reactions.to using hand tools: the resultant sounds and sights of thin wood shavings curling from a sharpened plane, the gentle hissing of the cutting blade, the solid note of a well-placed ax and the beauty of the clean chip flying to the ground, the elemental natural rhythm of the saw, and mallet on chisel, and rotation of a wood brace; all these are about to be lost, too. But they need not be. That brings us to the purposes of this book.

One purpose is to attempt to continue to some extent the traditions of intangible beauty found in handcraftsmanship in houses, furniture and other articles made of wood. Another is to record the techniques of using antique hand tools effectively before the dreary sameness of the technological age completely erases methods developed by human genius over a six-thousand-year span of history.

Still another purpose, perhaps of greater importance to our twentieth- and twenty-first-century societies than might be imagined, is to inspire modern man to experience the pleasure and satisfaction of creating beauty in wood with his hands and the tools his hands alone are capable of building.

Certainly, as the twentieth century heads into its last quarter, the time is ripe for a renaissance of hand craftsmanship. It will not come from industry because industry must, by its nature, think in terms of high volume and low cost, and machines are essential to meet these demanding criteria. Such a renaissance must come from the legions of home workshops found in the affluent society, where it well may play a manifold role. The hobbyist in woodworking might fulfill the purposes stated above, by preserving and recording the human values found in using hand tools. Of more importance, many people may with hand tools provide real meaning to their leisure.

Now, of course, there are a great many machines designed for the home workshop; bench saws and drill presses and power sanders and bench planers, some with a variety of auxiliary equipment suitable for doing many different jobs. We must be realistic about some of this equipment. It does replace the sometimes necessary apprentice of the old-time woodworking shop and serves his purpose in ripping boards to desired width and in taking much of the onerous, time-consuming labor of sanding from the arms and shoulders of the handcraftsmen. Machines, however, are designed for production, volume and duplication. In addition they are noisy, dangerous and often hostile. Surely they do most woodworking jobs ten times quicker than the same job is done with hand tools, but they also limit the choice of cuts and molding to the few designs thought suitable or saleable by the manufacturer. Machines lack the flexibility of hand tools and tend to make the worker more an operator than a craftsman; more the slave of the machine and its designer than the master of his tools.

The saving of time and labor is the usual rationale for using machine tools in home workshops, but such an argument is fallacious in many instances. Machines must be adjusted for almost every job. Often a small job can be done with a hand tool in the time taken to adjust the machine. As for labor, the craftsmen of olden times were as careful of their energy as modern, machine-age man. Using the old tools requires surprisingly little expenditure of energy when the right tool is chosen and the blades are sharp. One need not be afraid of them; he can concentrate on his creation rather than worry about his safety. Besides, the pleasure of their use is fully as satisfying as the exercise of tennis or handball or golf.

After all, one of the great problems of our age is to fill our leisure hours. As technology advances and computers perform the taxing mental gymnastics of our lives and working weeks become shorter and shorter, what are we to do with the increasing hours of spare time? Some of us might create beauty. To those who wish to use their mental and artistic abilities and respond to the challenges of how and why; to those who wish to exercise imagination and enjoy the human rhythms of sawing and planing and cutting with hand tools, craftsmanship can become a delightful pastime. It might well become even an obsession of sorts, but a most beneficent one. The use of hand tools is such a basic human activity that it teaches the user hidden secrets of the human mind and potential that can never be learned from a machine. When using hand tools a man can learn about himself.

The authority behind the techniques described in this book is necessarily based on experience rather than academic study. There aren't many books on the subject. The few books available, mostly outdated school texts or scholarly treatises on the uses of tools, offer a description of the tools themselves, their evolution over centuries of use or their manufacturers. Very little has been recorded about the actual use of the tools; the techniques needed. No one has told about the little things of how to hold them, how to stand, how to swing or push. It's much like the importance to a musician of learning the basic techniques of playing a violin or a guitar or a piano. There is a starting point in technique for tools, too.

One reason few writers have described the use of plane and saw and adz is because few living men, in the 1970s, have used them. The machine has dominated craftsmanship for several generations now, and the few old-time craftsmen left in the world are hard to find and usually more articulate with their hands than with either tongue or written word. They can demonstrate but cannot describe in words.

I shall attempt to fill this void. Since a boy I have been interested in the methods of early craftsmen, both primitive and civilized. For a long time, now, I have collected the tools of the handcraftsman, and collection led inevitably to use, and there the real pleasures of antique tools lay hidden. Techniques are not as durable items to collect as tools themselves, but they are infinitely more challenging to find and more fascinating to examine and far more an integral part of the character of a tool than any of its other aspects. Techniques, once learned, recapture the men of olden times, and nothing is more interesting or intriguing.

Circumstances in my life have fortunately coincided with

my interest in such matters. For one thing I grew up in the South, the depression South, a remnant of the "make do" South of poverty-stricken Reconstruction times. In this area the country craftsmen endured longer than in most other areas of the country. They had to for several reasons. There was not the expendable income available for expensive power tools, nor was there a market large enough in rural areas to justify mass production techniques. In addition, most of the craftsmen I have known while growing up lived in areas quite remote from modern hardware stores where they could shop for power tools, and most lacked electricity in their shops. Besides all this, most of my teachers over the years enjoyed the old ways. Perhaps I learned valuable attitudes from them as well as techniques.

All were able to visualize what they were trying to make or accomplish with wood. They all knew wood, and knew the properties of the various kinds of wood with which they worked. Such knowledge grew out of curiosity about the material and observation of how each wood behaved while being worked. None of my teachers ever quit learning, or ever lost the desire to learn. Being dependent on making tools and houses and furniture of wood, knowledge was a matter of survival, of course. Nevertheless, it is the key to becoming a good craftsman in wood.

Jim Whitley, who grew up in the upper settlement of Vinings, Georgia, now a suburban area of Atlanta, was my most versatile informant. He was born in 1873 in a log cabin built by his grandfather in 1842. Jim lived in the cabin until a couple of years before he died in 1962. Over the years he maintained the old pioneer cabin just as his father and grandfather did before him. All alone, he cut oak board trees, bucked them into suitable lengths, split them into billets and rived his own shingles when the old roof began to leak. In addition he made his own chairs on occasion, and he carved large dough bowls from billets of tulip poplar cut from his own trees.

Jim Whitley's most impressive triumphs in woodworking were the two or three fiddles he made after he had passed his seventieth birthday. He asked me one day if I could find a book on how violins were made, as he had always hankered to make a fiddle since he played one very well. I found a most comprehensive volume on the subject in the Atlanta Public Library and took it to him. He returned it a week later, prepared to start work on his first fiddle.

In the week he had the book he noted all the delicate measurements of the violins of Stradivarius. What's more, he duplicated all the special tools described and illustrated in the book. These included small compass planes, no more than three or four inches long, for smoothing the curved inside surfaces of back and belly, small inlay planes for decoration around the edge. Once prepared, Jim Whitley proceeded to make a beautiful violin with its back made of curly maple and belly made of spruce pine. The result was a professional job done by one who thoroughly understood his material, his tools and the techniques of using one or the other. Being able to watch him during the process was a fortunate experience for me.

Another important informant, who shall be mentioned later in this book, is my old friend and woods companion, Bryan Owle. The two of us used to camp and hunt together for as long as two weeks at a time in the wilderness of the Cherokee Indian Reservation in the North Carolina mountains. This was during the 1930s before that wild country was cut up with scenic highways and the sounds of the deep woods were drowned out by the roar of speeding automobiles.

Bryan Owle is an old-time woodsman. He, like Jim Whitley, also grew up in a log cabin, and he split his share of shingles while he was growing up. Mostly, however, he spent his time in the woods, hunting and trapping and logging, living off the country for as long as three months at a time. Being in the woods with him is a revelation which immeasurably broadens one's horizons of knowledge about trees and plants, beasts and birds and fishes. No tree in the woods passes his notice.

Not every tree in the woods, for instance, is suitable for board making, or for riving shingles with froe and maul. Bryan Owle, with his backwoods training, never fails to see and note a board tree when he passes one. Once when together we passed a huge sassafras, which grows two feet or more in diameter in the virgin wilderness. Bryan, trained to observe what might be useful in the woods, which are the grocery-hardware-building supply stores of the frontier, immediately mentioned that such a large sassafras would have been in demand during his youth for making oxbows. Sassafras is strong and close grained but surprisingly lightweight when dry, eminently suitable for the bows used in training young oxen.

There must never have been a better axman that Bryan Owle. The tool literally became part of him whenever he took it in his hands.

Bryan's area abounds in men who really know the woods. Ed Welch, a Cherokee who lives high up the mountain at the head of Wright's Creek, cleared ten acres of land with an ax, used the logs to build himself a house, two barns and a corncrib, and then cultivated the cleared land with horse and plow. All this occurred in the 1950s. Ed is one of the best board makers in the area, and thinks nothing of turning out a thousand hand split shingles a day after he has cut his tree and prepared his billets.

John Smith, a neighbor of Ed Welch, is a master wood-carver and greatly in demand for making tool handles for farmers and loggers in his area. This, too, takes more knowledge than most people can muster. The trees from which to make handles must be selected with care, seasoned properly, split carefully and shaped with precision.

There have been other sources of learning about the ways of working wood with hand tools. Watching the careful craftsmen at the Williamsburg restoration is a fine way to learn what must be done to result in the truly fine cabinetwork these artisans produce. A few glimpses of the handcraftsmen found in Italy and Spain have also added to my knowledge. In addition, the study of a few old, forgotten books has brought out little nuggets of knowledge which have been applicable to many of my own home workshop projects.

For instance, the reprint of Diderot's famous eighteenth century *Encyclopedia of Trades and Industries* illustrates most of the tools of handcraftsmanship in use, and has provided grounds for theory and experiment with the tools in my own collection. A quite obscure book published in England in 1904, illustrates and describes (sometimes poorly) the techniques of using many of the woodworking tools I once thought had disappeared several generations before the book was published. Then there have been a few old textbooks of the early twentieth century when shops were instituted as part of a complete curriculum in public schools. These have sometimes provided quite valuable hints on the easier use of some particular hand tool, saving many frustrating hours of experiment. The *Chronicle,* a quarterly publication of the Early American Industries Association, has yielded some extremely interesting and useful information of the tools available to the old-time craftsmen and the techniques of using these tools.

My best text in the use of old hand tools, however, has been my basement workshop. Over the years I have collected a variety of hand woodworking tools and have had others given to me. These include planes, adzes, axes, froes, augers and others more specialized in function. All these tools were acquired in usable condition or else they have been quite easily restored to usable condition. At times when I have needed a simple hand tool of old design which has not been available from antique dealers, I have made my own.

There are no power tools in my shop. With old hand tools, however, I have made desks and corner cabinets and paneled blanket chests. With a set of molding planes and a moving fillister I have made picture frame molding, coffee tables and small cabinets of various types, in addition to repairing antique furniture which sometimes required making a new part to fit the old construction. Indeed, I have also cut and bucked trees and even split a few shingles to see how it was done.

Making things by hand has opened up the adventure of using hand tools. Not only has it taught the techniques but it has also revealed the deep and very real emotional satisfaction of responding to the necessary rhythm of using hand tools, of inspecting each stroke of a plane and correcting any small errors with the next stroke.

I hope that this book may in some small measure encourage others with interests similar to mine to develop those interests, and perhaps to collect feelings lost with the handcraftsman as well as collecting his tools. Not only will the feelings bring satisfaction through a certain intangible, inexpressible beauty, but they will also lead to a greater appreciation of what we have in this day of power tools.

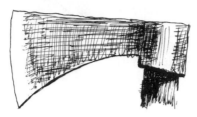

Axes—European

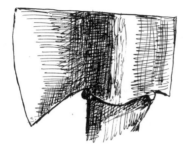

Double bit, American

Single bit, American design

Crosscut saws—three designs of teeth

CHAPTER I

The Ways of
Felling a Tree

FELLING is an art requiring great skill. It is also a science which must be applied to various sorts of trees as diverse in their individual characteristics as people. The ax, possibly the most ancient woodworking tool used by man, in the hands of a skilled woodsman becomes as much a precision instrument as a surgeon's scalpel. The two man crosscut saw was also widely used for felling in conjunction with the ax until the middle of the twentieth century.

At this time, soon after the technological advances of World War II were adapted by industry, the ancient ways of felling with ax and saw have become rapidly obsolete, and the ancient tools have been almost entirely replaced by the chain saw. The ruthless efficiency of this modern tool, after having been adopted for a generation, has for the most part extinguished the skilled axman. Still, the axman's instincts and methods are well worth recording. They show what a man is capable of doing with his hands and the simplest of tools.

In the vast forests of America during the formative years of the republic most felling was done entirely with an ax. There was good reason for this. Many of the early frontiersmen faced alone the needs of building cabins and rail fences and supplying firewood. There was no one to man the other end of a crosscut saw and what trees had to be cut were felled by one man. The ax was far more easily carried by one man traveling through "thickety" wilderness. Also, saws were made in Europe until after 1800 and were therefore expensive and limited in distribution.

The principles of felling are quite simple; the techniques, however, require great skill and stamina.

One of the guiding principles of felling is to control the direction in which a tree falls. This is done by means of two cuts or kerfs, on opposite sides of a tree trunk, each of them horizontal on the bottom and slanted at about a 45° angle at the top. The line where horizontal and oblique planes meet in the kerf should be exactly perpendicular to the direction in which the tree is intended to fall. The direction itself is controlled by the relative depth and position of the kerfs. The tree, all factors being equal, will fall on the side with the deeper and lower kerf.

The direction of felling a perfectly straight tree on a still day is decided upon by considering nearby trees which should be avoided in the falling, and deciding on a position where it can be conveniently bucked or cut into sections after being felled. Once this direction is determined the axman starts his work by cutting a kerf on the side opposite the direction the tree is desired to fall.

This first kerf should be cut about waist high to make it easier to have the bottom plane of the cut absolutely level. If it is not level, the tree will likely twist in falling and control over the direction of fall will be lost. The first cut should penetrate about two-fifths of the tree trunk's diameter.

When the first cut is made the axman starts his second on the opposite side. This cut, which causes the fall, should be made so that its bottom plane is two or three inches below the bottom plane of the first cut, the larger the tree the greater the difference in the levels of the two cuts. The axman must also be sure that the two cuts are exactly opposite each other so that the lines formed by the two angles are parallel.

The second, or felling, cut should be continued until it penetrates slightly under the first cut. At this time the axman will keep his ear tuned for the sound of rending fibers which anticipate the breaking of the small section of trunk still uncut and the falling of the tree. When the point of severance is reached the greater weight above the deeper cut creates the slight imbalance which brings the tree crashing spectacularly to the ground in the direction desired.

Here is the excitement of felling: the groaning of the re-

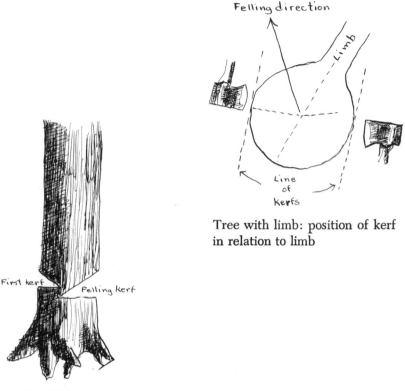

Felling direction

Limb

Line of Kerfs

Tree with limb: position of kerf
in relation to limb

First kerf

Felling kerf

Kerfs in felling a tree

sisting fibers as the felling cut finally penetrates almost to the
point of severance, the tree itself quivering more and more with
each blow; the final anguished cracking of the small remaining
unsevered section; the slow leaning of the trunk which accel-
erates as gravity begins to pull, and then the final popping of
the fibers and the roar of the limbs and foliage as the tree
plunges downward to fall with a crash on the leaf-covered floor
of the forest. Then all is quiet. Through the sunlight which
streams through the new opening in the forest ceiling float
motes of dust and a few leaves which were torn off as the cut
tree fell.

Few trees, if any, however, stand perfectly straight and perfectly balanced. Most are inclined one way or another by prevailing winds, or have a heavy branch on one side or are misshapen in some way which will affect the direction of the fall. Such expected abnormalities must be compensated for by the skill and instincts of the axman and the position of his cuts.

If, for instance, a tree has a heavy limb growing on one side, but not in the direction of the desired fall, the axman must position his notches in a manner that will use the weight of the trunk to counterbalance the weight of the limb. Instead of making the angle of his notch perpendicular to the direction of fall, he will position it so that it is instead perpendicular to an angle equal to the angle of the limb with the desired direction of fall. Then the tree will fall between the two angles. If the limb is particularly heavy and long, the axman may cut his first notch only one-fifth through the diameter of the tree with the felling notch penetrating four-fifths of the diameter.

Sometimes a tree to be cut will lean so heavily in the wrong direction for felling that no compensation of the leaning weight can be made with even the deepest felling cut. In such a situation the axman may resort to the use of a spring pole.

A spring pole is no more than a straight, springy sapling, three to four inches in diameter at the butt and twelve to fifteen feet long, stripped of all branches. To use it the axman, after cutting a shallow first notch in the tree, cuts an additional shallow notch some eight or ten feet from the ground on the leaning side of the tree. If a properly placed limb is found this far from the ground it may serve in place of a notch. The top of the spring pole is then inserted in the notch or under the limb and the pole is pulled from the middle to form an arc, its convex curve toward the tree. While the spring pole is so held a stout stake is driven into the ground against its butt. Then the felling kerf, opposite the pole, is cut deeper than usual. When the trunk is nearly severed the spring of the pole will push the tree over in the desired direction of fall.

Almost every tree to be felled presents different problems to the axman with solutions coming only from experience. The old-time axman who cut the tremendous trees of the Southern Appalachians, the virgin long-leaf pine of the southern coastal

Use of spring pole

plains and who cleared the dense forests of Wisconsin and Michigan, developed an uncanny control over the tree he felled. It is said, indeed, that an old timer could plant a stake where he wanted a misshapen tree to fall, then fell the tree with such accuracy that it could drive the stake into the ground.

There is no difference in principle involved in felling with either ax or crosscut saw. When using the crosscut the felling notch is cut first at least one-third through the diameter of the trunk. Then the saw is started opposite the notch and two or three inches below the horizontal plane of the notch. Sometimes, when using a saw, the tree sways slightly, pinching the saw blade and making it immobile. Two solutions to this problem are available: a small, thin wedge of iron or hardwood may be driven into the saw cut, behind the blade, opening it up so that the saw will slide freely; kerosene, or other lubricant, may be applied to the saw blade.

It is really more convenient and quicker to fell smaller trees, up to two feet in diameter, entirely with an ax. With larger trees, however, the kerf of an ax must be so large that a great deal of potential lumber is wasted in chips.

After a tree is felled it must be bucked, or segmented into lengths of from six to twenty feet, to be transported to the sawmill. In the days before the internal combustion engine, logs were generally bucked in longer lengths than in recent years. The logs were dragged by oxen or hauled to the sawmill by lumber carts, merely strong axles between huge, heavy wheels of six foot diameter. One end of the log was lashed to the axle and the other dragged on the ground as the cart was pulled by a team of mules or oxen. Where logs were floated to the mill on rivers, the length might be limited somewhat, depending on the size of the river. Motor trucks, however, seldom carry logs of more than twelve to sixteen feet.

Saw logs have almost always been bucked with a crosscut saw, again because an ax kerf is wasteful of good lumber. There is no difficulty of technique in bucking with the saw unless the log settles, pinching the blade. Here again a small iron or wooden wedge is knocked into the top of the saw kerf to free the blade.

Bucking with an ax on any size log, from six inches in diameter up, does require special techniques and special agility. The two faces of the kerf are cut at the same slant, forming an angle of about 45° where they meet in the exact center of the log. Instead of starting his cut on the top of the log, as does the sawyer, the axman cuts two kerfs, one on each side, which meet in the middle on a line exactly perpendicular to the ground. To do this he must stand on top of the log and bend almost double perhaps to reach the wood close to the ground.

While the same type ax is used for felling and bucking, axmen who buck large logs might use an ax equipped with a longer-than-usual handle to reach the bottom of the kerf on logs three feet or more thick.

Axes, as with any other precision tool, are interesting in themselves. The evolution of the ax from the crude instrument of the Stone Age to the well-balanced double-bit ax of the nineteenth century American lumberman has been well docu-

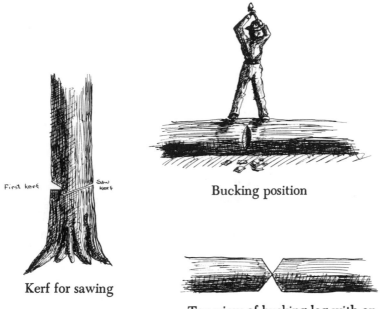

First kerf Saw kerf

Bucking position

Kerf for sawing

Top view of bucking log with ax

mented in a number of sources. A brief review of this history is in order to explain the techniques of using the tool most efficiently.

The earliest axes found are similar in design and construction to the ancient weapon and tools of the Saxons, a name which is said to derive from the long-bladed axes they used primarily as weapons. This fearful item was made by doubling a strip of wrought iron to form an eye with overlapping ends, then welding the overlap together with a piece of carbon steel* welded between the ends to serve as the bit. There was no poll or specially formed butt end to the Saxon ax. In later centuries the woodcutters of Europe modified this weapon for woodcutting by shortening the blade and making the eye heavier, creating better balance and providing more durability.

In twentieth century Portugal, where there have never

Carbon steel is a modern term but in this context it best describes the type of refined iron ore the Saxons crudely developed.

been great forests to challenge the genius of axsmiths, the design of axes made in modern factories and used in clearing are almost identical in form with the ancient Saxon ax, with long blade, small eye and straight edge. In the forested countries, however, such as England, France, Germany and the Scandinavian nations, the more efficient felling ax was developed. This form has persisted to some extent in Europe and in areas of recent European empires. For instance, the São Paulo [Brazil] factory of the Collins Ax Company, an American enterprise, continued to make felling axes of exactly the same design as sixteenth century European axes for the South American market until the last half of the twentieth century. Even though Brazil was a Portuguese possession until early in the nineteenth century, the heavy woodlands of the Amazon Valley required a better tool for clearing and lumbering than the traditional Portuguese ax. The felling axes used there had a shorter blade, a larger, heavier eye and, of utmost importance, a curved edge which penetrates far easier than a straight edge.

In pre-colonial America, with its varied climates and woodlands similar to those of ancient Europe and Britain, gave final impetus to the development of the ax. Here the old felling ax of Europe was modified by adding a poll to the back of the eye, finally giving the tool the balance needed to make it into a precision instrument. Perhaps this final evolution of the ax came about because in colonial America the blacksmith, who made the axes, was himself required to chop down trees in frontier areas and he realized the disadvantages of an improperly balanced ax. Later, about 1850, the needs of the professional lumbermen who cleared millions of acres of timberland brought about the design of the double-bit ax.

Warriors of olden days used double-bit axes and so did Scandinavian woodcutters. But the Americans were the first to develop it as a fine precision tool. Its balance is almost perfect, and the thinness of its blade gives it far more penetrating ability than the heavier blades of older designs.

There are two main reasons for the ax being a fine tool which can be used with remarkable precision: balance and weight.

Unless the blade is aimed to penetrate the wood where the

axman wants, then many blows will be wasted. After centuries of evolution and refinement the American ax provides such excellent balance that the head merely has to be swung in the proper arc to bring its sharpened edge to a desired place on the tree being felled or bucked.

Accuracy is only one aspect of chopping, however. The blade must also penetrate as far as possible with each blow, and this requires a curved edge and weight; but not too much weight to tire the axman unduly by lifting the ax for each blow. Part of the genius of primitive man when he developed basic tools was his instinctive understanding of how to make simple weight work for him, not against him. This instinct has been somewhat dulled in modern man because he has so many sources of power which can take the place of weight in operating tools. Modern man can call on pneumatic power, steam, electricity or internal combustion. Primitive man had only weight and muscle. His tools were designed to give him maximum power from these elements.

Axes have always been available in a variety of weights to fit different purposes and different people. Camping axes, where weight is a factor in transport, usually weigh about 2½ pounds. Other axes, single or double-bit, range upward in weight to about six pounds, the preference of most of the old-time professional lumberjacks and frontiersmen who cleared the great American forests. Many of the old woodsmen, indeed, carried a six-pound ax on long hunting and trapping expeditions, preferring the extra burden of transport in order to enjoy the added efficiency of a heavy ax for chopping, once they had established a base camp. The choice was simply a matter of whether to expend a little more energy in carrying the extra weight into the wilderness or to be required to expend much effort with each blow in using a lighter ax for chopping. Actually, carrying extra weight is better, for even the strongest man cannot make a lightweight ax penetrate tough oak or hickory or heart pine without breaking the ax handle. Human muscle simply cannot substitute adequately for weight. Light axes are only suitable for light work.

Certain aspects of handles are extremely important in proper and efficient use of the ax. The function of the handle is

only to guide the weight and balance of the ax head. Hickory
has always been the choice material for American ax handles
and southern American white hickory is shipped all over the
world for the manufacture of ax and other tool handles. Before
America was discovered the Europeans used ash for ax handles,
and in the north woods of America or Europe where hickory
and ash do not always grow, maple makes a fair substitute.
Choice of wood is important because a good ax handle must be
strong, smooth, light and springy.

The ax handle began in ancient times as a straight helve,
shaped to an oval section to fit the hand comfortably so as to
avoid tiring the hand during a long day of chopping. In America, about 1850, this straight handle was modified into a graceful
curve with either a doe foot or a colt foot end. The curve helped
place the axe edge more accurately; the swelling end made it
easier to hold loosely, without its slipping through a palm lubricated with good honest sweat from the axman's exertions.

Until recent times, when mass production began to domi-
nate craftsmanship, the good axman designed his own ax handle
to fit his physical characteristics and his personality. Virtually all
kept a pattern of a handle the design of which had been developed with many a weary blow over the years.

Since the handle is used only to control the direction and
weight of the ax head, it should be quite slim and springy. Any
experienced axman can for months use a handle broken halfway
through as long as there is enough left to guide the head without
twisting. Most handles used by old timers were not more than
1½ inches thick where they were slimmed under the ax eye before
it began swelling to fit the hand. Though curved handles were
usually preferred for the single-bit felling ax, the double-bit
felling ax developed in America about 1850 always required a
straight handle.

The length of an efficiently designed ax handle is fully as
important as its other aspects. Length is a relative factor and
must fit the axman. Generally each man can decide the proper
length for his own personal handle by placing the ax head upside down between his feet and letting his arms hang loosely.
His handle is then cut to match the distance between the top of
the ax, where it rests on the floor, and the point where the heels

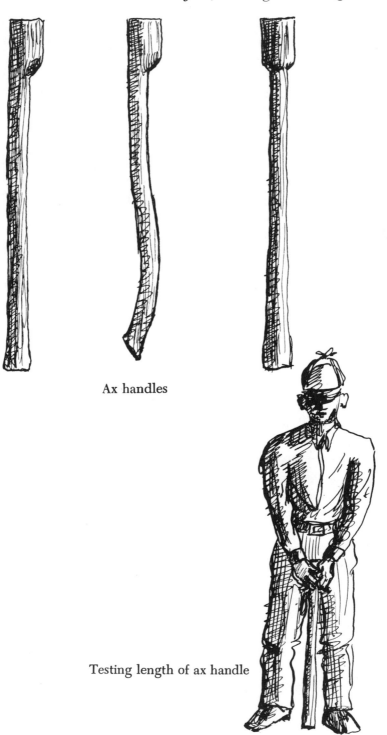

Ax handles

Testing length of ax handle

of his hands meet the wrists. Experience sometimes modifies
this slightly, but it is a good starting place in determining the
length of the handle.

Sometimes an extra short handle may be needed for chopping in thick brush. At other times a very long handle is needed
to fell or buck giant trees such as redwoods or the huge six- and
eight-foot diameter oaks and chestnuts and tulip poplars still
found occasionally in secluded coves of the Southern Appalachians. On these large trees a normal handle would not extend
the reach of an axman enough to remove wood in the center of
the cut, some three or four feet from the axman.

When handles are abnormally short or long for special work
the good axman remembers that the difference in leverage
offered also changes the weight requirements of the ax head.
An extra heavy head should be used on a short handle to make
up for lack of momentum effected by the head swinging in a
short arc; conversely, the extra-long handle provides more
momentum in the swing, but makes the ax head more difficult
to lift because of a disadvantage in leverage. Therefore, longer
handles theoretically use lighter heads.

An illustration of the principle involved in the ratio of ax
head weight and length of handle is a comparison of the quite
common belt ax sold for campers and the tomahawk of the backwoods. The small ax has about a 1½ to 2 pound head with
usually a handle of about fifteen inches. It is practically useless
for anything but splitting kindling, for it lacks the leverage and
the weight to chop a tree any larger than one which may be cut
with a sharp hunting knife. The old-fashioned tomahawk, however, is far more efficient. Although its head generally weighed
no more than a pound, its handle was usually at least two feet
long, and the extra leverage gained by the additional nine
inches on the handle makes it a far more effective tool for light
chopping than the belt ax.

As an integral part of an ax, the handle must fit properly
into the eye of the head. First of all it must be exactly parallel
with the vertical axis of both poll and cheeks. Also, it must fit
precisely and tightly.

Handles, where they fit into the eye, are usually scraped
with a piece of broken glass to the precise dimension needed so

Checking straightness of handle

that the eye section can be slid into the eye tightly. It is secured by driving a slim hardwood wedge into the end of the eye section. When the handle is seated and wedged the axman should hold the handle knob between both hands and check to see that the line of the edge is exactly centered and exactly parallel to the long axis of the handle. If these requirements are not met the relation of the head and handle may be adjusted by driving small iron or wooden wedges into the end of the eye section of the handle.

Sometimes ax handles break and must be replaced, often in the woods. The eye section of a broken handle is easily removed with a small fire. First, a shallow ditch is dug in the ground and a fire built in this ditch. When the fire is burning steadily the double-bit ax head is placed flat so that its eye is over the fire, its blade, or blades, resting on the ground on each side of the fire. The blades are then covered with damp earth, piled on the bit to a depth of 1 to 1½ inches. This protects the temper of the bit from being softened further by heat conducted from the eye. Once the eye has heated to the point that it burns the wood in the eye, the ax head is removed from the fire, the section of the broken handle pushed out, and the eye cooled so that a new handle may be inserted.

Single-bit axes may have a broken handle burned from the eye by driving the bit into the ground to the level of the eye and building a small fire over the eye and poll.

If, as a woods' expedient, a new handle must be made of green wood, then the axman secures it with a wedge some two or three inches longer than usual. The butt of this wedge will be left protruding, and as the green wood shrinks the wedge will be driven farther into its end.

Weight, balance, length of handle and shape of cutting edge of the felling ax is of no consequence unless the edge is sharp.

Ax edges properly tempered are relatively soft. They must be hard enough to cut through pine knots, for instance, but never so hard and brittle that the knot will chip pieces from the ax edge. At such a temper they are quite easily sharpened, particularly if the edge is maintained with adequate sharpening to keep it from becoming blunt.

The tools for ax sharpening are the file and the stone. To sharpen a single-bit ax in the woods without benefit of work bench, vise or special jig to secure the ax head while being sharpened, the axman makes his own holdfast by chopping an acute angled notch, about 30°, in a convenient log. This notch should be wide enough at its mouth to accommodate the poll. When the notch is prepared, the ax is driven pollfirst into the notch as far as possible. This will hold it steady. Then the edge is formed with a ten- or twelve-inch mill bastard file, filing away from the edge on one side and then the other.

New axes must sometimes be filed quite severely to form

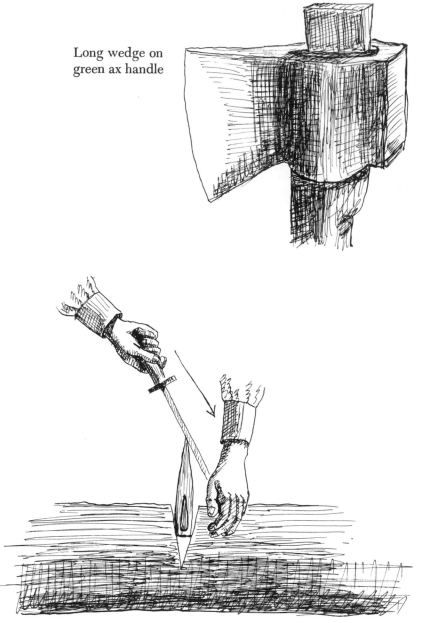

Long wedge on
green ax handle

Sharpening in the woods

Position of double bit ax for sharpening

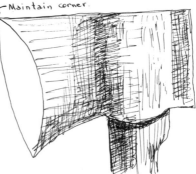

Plane of sharpening

Maintain corner.

the desirable 15° to 20° angle, on the edge, depending on the hardness of the wood to be chopped. A careful axman will take the pains to file the rounded cheeks of a new ax blade to flat surfaces which meet to form the edge. This will leave a half-moon-shaped flat surface on each cheek. As the edge is filed it is also shaped, if necessary, to the proper curve. Care must be taken in the initial sharpening as well as in subsequent maintenance to preserve a sharp corner at the junction of the curved edge and the top of the ax head.

In filing one should always have a handle, homemade or bought, on the file. In addition, it is wise to place a small guard, about one inch round or square, made of thin sheet metal, copper preferred, or thin wood, over the file tang between the heel of the file and the handle. If this precaution is not taken even the most careful fellow may slip while filing and deeply slice the heel of his hand on the newly sharpened edge.

After filing, the ax edge is further refined by sharpening it to a depth of $\frac{1}{32}$ of an inch at a slightly wider angle, say 25°. Some will then hone the edge with a fine-grained stone, but this is considered by most to be superfluous attention. Stones, usually circular and designated ax stones, are used in a rotating motion while pressed lightly against the edge. Care must be taken in using the stone to see that the heel of the hand or the ends of fingers do not protrude over the bottom surface of the stone, creating the possibility of a bad cut if flesh and newly sharpened edge meet.

Once an ax has been filed properly the edge is easily maintained by touching it up with the stone about once an hour of chopping. Sharpening is so effortless once an edge is formed, and a sharp edge makes the labor of chopping so much easier, that only a fool will neglect to take a stone with him whenever he uses an ax for an hour or more.

The sharpening of double-bit axes is only slightly different from that of the single-bit variety. Usually one edge of a double-bit is sharpened with the two halfmoon planes of the single-bit. The other generally is filed to a relatively obtuse angle of 30° only along the curve of the edge. One bit may then be used for felling, its opposite reserved for cutting through hard knots and for splitting. Too, the curve of the edge of most double-bit axes is an even arc formed on a line which bisects the head perpendicular to the eye. This curve must be maintained in its original arc as with the single-bit tool.

Double-bit axes require no holdfast while being sharpened in the woods. One bit may be merely driven upright in a convenient log or stump while the other edge is sharpened. Then the position is reversed.

Regardless, however, of the ways to notch a tree, the proper juxtaposition of the notches to control its fall, the fine balance and the weight of the ax head, all these factors together will not make even one mark on a tree. A tree is felled and bucked only by a man at the end of the ax handle, using the ax head to remove wood in the proper places to make the tree fall.

The techniques of using an ax are simple in principle, but require a great deal of practice to be effective. In addition, factors which may adversely affect these techniques must be observed and corrected before chopping begins.

One important factor is the presence of limbs and undergrowth within a radius of the axman's shoulder and the head of the ax. It is most important to cut these potential hindrances out of the way before starting to chop. Otherwise the ax head may

Clearing under brush before chopping

be deflected by a small branch, making the axman lose control
of his ax and perhaps causing the edge to hit him in the head or
on a leg.

An important consideration in using an ax tirelessly is the
stance of the axman. He should stand facing the side of the tree
to be cut, his feet spread about two feet apart to provide stability. Then, if he is right handed, the left foot should be moved
forward about six or eight inches. He should be far enough from
the tree so that the ax blade, when the tool is held in his out-
stretched arms, will meet the center of the tree.

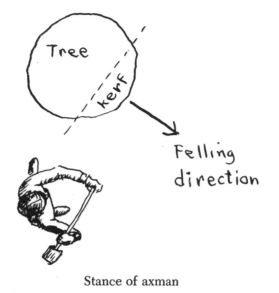

Stance of axman

For bucking, the axman must stand on the fallen log with his feet spread about two feet apart. The kerf is cut midway between his feet.

There are four distinct movements to chopping with an ax: lifting, swinging, disengaging and recovery. These movements become so instinctive with minimum practice that it is sometimes difficult to separate them and, indeed, one movement flows into another with no break, a harmony of coordination which is as elementally satisfying as it is efficient.

In lifting, the handle is grasped loosely but securely in the left hand just above the knob or colt's foot. The right hand grasps the handle loosely but securely just below the head, making the weight of the head easy to lift. The right hand then lifts the head into the pre-swing position, holding it at the proper height to cut the proposed kerf and in a position which places the line of the edge parallel to the intended cut. When lifting is finished the right arm should be as far back of the head as it can comfortably be placed with the elbow slightly bent. The left arm is straight, with the hand in front of the right shoulder.

In swinging, both hands actuate the arc of the ax head. The

Four positions of chopping

left hand remains in its position at the end of the handle during the swing, but the right hand slides down the handle until it reaches a position above the left hand just as the edge of the ax bites into the wood.

To disengage the ax edge wedged crosswise into the tough cut fibers of the wood, the axman slides his right hand midway up the handle to serve as a fulcrum, then pushes the knob to the left, thereby levering the edge out of the cut. Once the kerf is well started the handle must be given a counterclockwise twist after each blow at the top of the kerf. This splits off the chips within the kerf. Then the ax head is brought back to its starting position in the recovery movement which consists of sliding the right hand up the handle, lifting as it slides, until once more the ax head is ready to swing.

When starting to cut it is better to make the lower horizontal cut first, as it is easier to twist out the chip in the angled upper cut.

The axman soon learns to use his right arm to provide most of the power of the swing, the left hand and arm being used primarily to control direction and angle of the cut.

The kerf is started with two blows no more than six to eight vertical inches apart, as this is about the largest chip which can be removed with a six-pound ax. The bottom, horizontal cut is always on the same plane as the preceding cut. As the kerf deepens, however, it must be made wider by making the upper, oblique cuts higher and higher. On large trees the axman usually cuts two kerfs, one directly above the other. When each has reached the same depth he splits out the wood between the two, joining them into one, and proceeds as before.

Other problems on dislodging chips appear as the kerf penetrates deeper into the tree. At a certain point the chips to be removed attain a width of perhaps three times the width of the ax bit. When this point is reached the axman devotes six blows, three at the bottom and three at the top of each chip in a particular order; the outside cuts, top and bottom, are made first; next the two bottom cuts are joined with a cut in the center and, last, the two top cuts are joined and the chip split off simultaneously with the last blow of the series.

Nothing, not even a Nureyev or a running deer, is more graceful than an expert axman intent on felling or bucking a tree with an ax suited to his size and physique. The easy stance, the twisting motion of powerful shoulders, the precision of swinging arms constitute a natural ballet done in one position. The ax is like a flying bird of prey, the chips its victims, making a fragrant carpet of creamy wood on the forest floor. Accompaniment for the dance is the regular, precise beat of the ax as it hits and penetrates the resonant tree trunk, its grand finale being the roaring, crashing, cracking sounds of the tree falling in its predetermined arc to the ground.

Bryan Owle, who lives near Soco Gap in the Great Smoky Mountains, provided a fine example of such art when in his prime, before World War II. A woodsman of the old school,

Six blows on large chips

Bryan spent most of his life in the woods, hunting, trapping, logging and plain woods loafing. He grew up on virtually a frontier farm on Goose Creek near Cherokee, North Carolina, living in a two story log cabin built by his father. He grew up with an ax in his hand.

Bryan always carried a double-bit six-pound ax when he went to the woods, even though he might backpack the weight as far as twenty miles into the rugged roadless Smokies of his younger days. Once, for a two-week period, he used an ax that had its handle split from the eye to within twelve inches of the knob, the remaining sound section being no more than half an inch through. Yet, with this damaged handle, he could fell a foot-thick hickory in fifteen to twenty minutes and buck it into six foot-long lengths for the fire in another twenty minutes. His secret was in his precision which allowed him to throw out chips as big as a dinner plate and an inch thick. His blows were so accurately placed that his cuts looked as though they had been sliced with one stroke of a giant razor.

Bryan never seemed to hurry. His rhythmic blows were slow and seemingly effortless, the well-placed ax doing his work as he directed it through the handle. When finished he was never even out of breath. His kind began to disappear shortly after World War II when the chain saw became the universal logger's tool all over the world.

One of the elemental secrets of using hand woodworking tools was exposed in Bryan Owle's skill at using an ax, the fundamental woodworking tool. His attitude was that the tool should do the work with minimum effort on his part. In turn, he maintained the tool properly, using it only for its purpose, keeping it sharp and never allowing it to go into the ground. The same attitude should be directed at all woodworking tools; planes, adzes, saws, chisels, and others.

The other basic tool for felling and bucking trees, the cross-cut saw, is neither as exciting nor as satisfying to use as a good ax. It is, however, an efficient tool and its use requires well-defined techniques.

Saws, though not as ancient as the ax, have a most respectable pedigree in the genealogy of tools. They were used in Egypt five thousand years ago, and archaeological investigations have found Stone Age saws made of wood with saw teeth of stone or shark's teeth fastened to the wood with various types of gum. The saws of Egypt were made of bronze and iron and the basic design did not change until the late eighteenth century.

Early saws were merely bands of steel with 1 to 1½ teeth per inch filed into one side. The blade was operated by an upright handle fastened to each end.

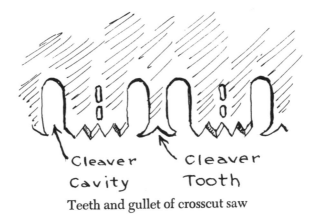

Cleaver   Cleaver
Cavity   Tooth

Teeth and gullet of crosscut saw

A crosscut saw is designed to cut transversely through the fibers of a tree, requiring that each tooth be a separate cutting instrument which fulfills its function successively as the saw is drawn back and forth. To accomplish this the teeth must be of exactly the same height and they must be filed so that each angled edge is sharpened into a knife blade, a sharp point ensuing where the two edges meet. Successive teeth are filed on opposite sides so that the points of any two adjacent teeth will have the thickness of the saw blade between them. The teeth are set before using, which means that each tooth is bent toward the side opposite the filed edge at about a 10° angle, widening the distance separating the points of adjacent teeth. Set is necessary in a saw to widen the kerf slightly so that the blade can move easily without sticking within the kerf.

As the saw is drawn back and forth the teeth slice through the wood fibers in two parallel cuts. The wood particles between these cuts, the sawdust, is automatically removed by the action of the saw.

In the late nineteenth century in America, and presumably in other countries of the world, the ancient, simple design of saw teeth was altered. The new saw works on exactly the same principle as the ancient Egyptian saw. Instead of a continuous row of cutting teeth, though, it has a number of series of cutting teeth down the length of the blade, each series consisting of from two to four teeth, separated by chisel teeth which somewhat resemble the zodiacal sign of Aries, and gullets, or deep round-ended notches as wide as the teeth. The chisel, or cleaner, teeth are designed to clean out the particles of wood between the parallel slices of the cutting teeth. Because of these chisel teeth, the dust created by a sharp saw of the new design is not dust but small triangular shavings of cross-grained wood. For this reason the new saw is more efficient than the old.

Crosscut saws may be sharpened in the woods with a file, as with axes. Sharpening consists of two actions, jointing, or filing all teeth to exactly the same height, and sharpening. Jointing is quite important to efficient sawing because those teeth lower than others do no work, and the labor of operating the saw increases accordingly.

Sharpening may be done with a ten-inch mill bastard file, filing away from the edge at a 30° angle for the cutting teeth. Chisel teeth should be filed straight across the top of the chisel edge so that the jointing will not be altered. The chisel edge should be kept at exactly the level of the points of the cutting teeth.

Although the two-man crosscut saw is far more monotonous to use than the ax, it does require a technique, which, once developed, makes sawing easier. Again a good stance is required. The sawyers should stand with the saw at their respective right hands and face the saw at a 45° angle. The handles are gripped with the left hand next to the saw blade and the right hand above the left. Feet are spread two feet apart.

For sawing the stance must be varied at times to suit the vagaries of topography and other factors found in the woods. At times the sawyers must kneel, with one knee on the ground. In felling, it is necessary for both sawyers to stand on the same side of the saw, one facing to his right, the other to his left. Since the man facing to his left will have to use his left arm more,

Holding position of saw

the two sawyers may change positions from time to time during the day.

Two-man saws are invariably pulled alternately by each sawyer; they are never pushed, which causes the thin blade to buckle. As one sawyer pulls, the other keeps his grip on the handle but moves his hands and arms forward at the established speed of the tool, neither pushing nor holding back.

A sawyer who holds back is said to be "riding the saw," making it more difficult for his partner to pull. The classic joke about riding concerns an experienced sawyer saying to his neophyte associate, "Look, I don't so much mind you riding the saw, but please don't drag your feet."

The power for sawing comes from the whole upper body and to some extent the legs, rather than solely from the arms.

Sawing, too, is a graceful sight to watch. A good sense of rhythm is absolutely essential for the two sawyers to coordinate their movements precisely. Also, the sound of the saw is soothing; ripping wood fiber and the high pitched ringing of the tempered steel blade. As each man pulls, a stream of sawdust flows from the kerf alternately at each side to form a cone of wood particles on the ground.

Before the advent of chain saws, which have now placed the crosscut saw in the limbo of history, most hardware stores also sold one-man crosscut saws. These consist of a blade some four feet long with a carpenter-type enclosed saw handle riveted or screwed to one end, and above this an upright handle. The right hand is put in the big handle, while the upright handle is clasped by the left hand. One-man saws have blades thick enough so that they can be both pulled and pushed. Smaller versions of the one-man saw are the wooden framed bucksaw, once a farmyard standby for sawing firewood, and the metal-framed bow saw, a twentieth century affair.

But now, expectantly, as this book is being written, the age of Aquarius is being born. Apparently Aquarius will be an age of dominant technology, despite the fact that its zodiacal origin was conceived in the dimness of prehistory when hand tools, too, were first conceived. Its anticipated progress will most certainly offer more and faster production but it could completely eliminate the axman, the sawyer, and all the grace and natural rhythm and animal satisfaction of felling a tree with ax and saw.

The chain tools which replace the ax and the crosscut saw do nothing to replace the human values, and the purely human skills and human dignity of the venerable axman and sawyer. Chain saws are dangerous, unpleasant creations, noisy and smelly and dependent not upon human muscles but only on a source of fuel. Those who use them are not dignified by a proud and specific title; they are called merely chain saw operators, slaves to the religion of progress and technology, and perhaps to the machines themselves.

There is, however, some slim hope offered to the memory of the axman and the sawyer. Maybe Aquarius will bring with it such a host of affluent householders that each can afford a fireplace. If this becomes true then perhaps these householders will rediscover the independence of productive exercise in using ax and saw to prepare their own cords of firewood. They will find this ancient exercise far more satisfying than jogging and weight lifting. Many, indeed, may discover that perfecting the precision of using an ax properly can possibly improve the golf game.

CHAPTER II

Splitting

Most varieties of trees favor man by growing in parallel fibers which may be separated rather easily by splitting, if the man has the proper tools and knows his wood. In splitting, knowledge is as much a tool as any other factor.

Over the millennia, man in many various cultures has used the splitting process to shape the trunks and sections of trunks into a host of useful items and components by the basically simple process of splitting. Wood split to varying degrees has been used for fence posts and rails, shingles, laths for plaster walls, clapboards, fence palings, puncheon benches and floors and other things. Splitting as a basic step in forming wood only disappeared as a whole after World War II when men familiar with splitting had been almost entirely displaced by sawmill men. In the latter years of the twentieth century one still finds a few split rail fences, and a few boardmakers to furnish hand-split shingles, but many of the fences are formed with a hydraulic splitting machine and sold through lumber yards and garden supply outlets at a fabulous price.

Not every type of tree is suitable for splitting, and not every tree within a suitable species will conform to the desires of the workman. And some trees which split easily are not durable enough to be used for purposes in which the article is exposed to weather or dampness or buried in the earth. Oak has always been known for its durability, but not every type of oak is suitable for all the uses of split items. And some trees, though they split easily, do not split smoothly, having long splinters or

Post sunk small end in the ground

deep troughs in the split surface so that they may be used only for limited purposes.

Here is a list of the most suitable trees for different items made of split wood:

For Fence Posts:

Yellow Locust	Chestnut Oak
Cedar	Chestnut
Cypress	Walnut (once plentiful enough to
Post Oak	be squandered on mundane items)

Yellow locust, cedar and chestnut may be expected to last in the ground for from 75 to 100 years; the oaks and walnut may be expected to last for from 25 to 50 years, if cut in the winter and seasoned before being sunk. Folklore dictates that the top end of the split section be put in the ground for longevity. If the portion to be sunk is charred on its surface before being sunk, rot and termites will be greatly discouraged.

In the drier areas of the West almost any type tree may be used for fence posts.

For Fence Rails:
     All of the above, plus:
     Red Oak   Heart Pine
     Scarlet Oak   Black Oak

These trees may be used for the rails in post-and-rail fences. Only the types used for fence posts should be utilized for the rails of a worm fence.

For Shingles:
     Cypress   Chestnut
     Cedar   Chestnut Oak
     White Oak   Red Oak
     Tulip Poplar   Pine

Cypress and cedar will last on a roof for up to a hundred years; white oak, chestnut oak and chestnut for from 50 to 75 years; pine, red oak and tulip poplar for from 20 to 25 years. Pine generally is used on small outbuildings which can be re-roofed completely without much work.

For Clapboards:
     White Oak   Post Oak
     Red Oak   Chestnut Oak

Other trees may be used for sawn clapboards but only those listed above can be split properly to form clapboards, which are thinner on one edge. (This will be explained later in this chapter.)

Fence Palings, Laths and Tobacco Sticks:
     Pine   Chestnut
     Cedar   Cypress
     White Oak   Red Oak
     Post Oak

Pine, however, is the favorite for tobacco sticks because it is so easily split with an ax.

Ship and Boat Strakes:
    White Oak
    Chestnut Oak
    Post Oak

Tool handles:
    White Hickory
    Ash
    Maple

Trees used for ax, hammer and peavy handles should generally be small, no more than eight inches in diameter. The precise ax handle maker, however, will cut a tree large enough to split out handle planks which have the radial grain running parallel to the long axis of the cross section. This prevents warping. A tree from six to eight inches in diameter will allow this.

There are a few trees that simply will not split and should be avoided:

Beech	Box Elder
Elm	Wild Cherry
Ironwood (Hornbeam)	Sourwood
Buckeye	Sycamore

Fortunately, none of these hard-to-split trees are suitable for shingles, fence posts, rails, etc. Some are beautiful woods, however, and may be shaped by cutting to produce all manner of handsome objects.

Among the great variety of hand woodworking tools which man inherited from his prehistoric ancestors, the tools for splitting are few and simple. First of all, as with any facet of woodworking, is that premier tool, the ax. Some axes split wood with less effort than others, the American single-bit ax being the best and the thin-bladed felling ax of ancient Europe being the most difficult with which to split.

The Germans who settled in Pennsylvania and other eastern states brought with them an ingenious tool designed only for splitting. They called it a *holzaxt*, though it is not a cutting ax, being useless for felling or bucking. Actually the *holzaxt* is a heavy iron or steel wedge pierced like an ax for a handle. With its weight and obtuse edge it splits large logs far more easily than an ax and its heavy poll may be used as a sledge to drive in iron wedges when splitting a long log. In the South it is called either a splitting ax or a go-devil.

A good axman can do a fine, clean job of splitting on a straight-grained log with one ax if the log is no longer than six or eight feet, or with two axes on a longer log. Of course, two axmen with good eyes can greatly facilitate the job. Two *holzaxts* can serve as well.

Splitting always starts at an end, preferably the smaller. Sighting off the core of the log the axman swings his blade directly above his head and drives it into the log as hard as possible some three or four inches from the end. Depending on the diameter of the log and the type tree this first blow sometimes will split the log through. If it does not the ax is removed and driven again into the started split until the split penetrates the diameter.

Often the ax will become so tightly wedged in the log that it cannot be removed without danger of breaking the handle. When this occurs another ax, its handle opposite that of the first, is driven into the split at the end of the log. The wedging action of the second ax will open the split enough to loosen the first and allow its withdrawal.

Once the split extends through the diameter of the log the rest is easy, as long as the ax handler has a good eye and a straight handle The first ax is left in the split, keeping it open. The second ax, its handle away from the split, is then driven into the extremity of the split, which usually extends from two to three feet beyond the first ax, depending on the thickness and type of log.

Now loosened, the first ax is withdrawn and driven into the split as close as the axman's skill allows to the head of the second ax, which loosens it so that it may be withdrawn and again driven into the extremity of the split. The process is repeated until the two halves of the log are separated. Each half is then split in the same manner.

Quarter logs are similarly split, but quarters must often be braced so that the bark is held parallel to the ground. This is done easily with three or four stakes driven into the ground.

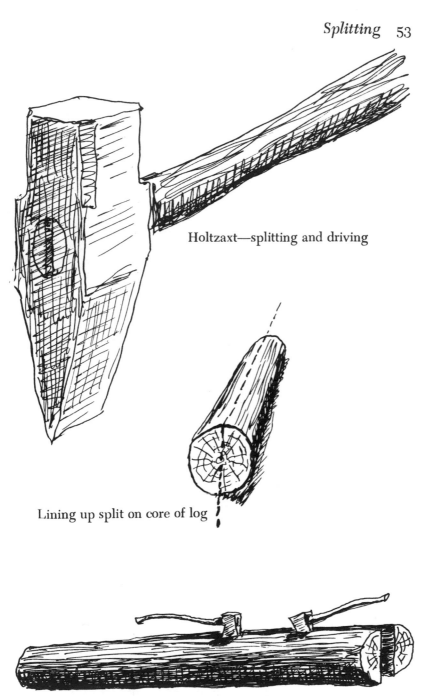

Holtzaxt—splitting and driving

Lining up split on core of log

Using two axes to split log

Short billets of fireplace or shingle length are easily split with one ax if the billet is no more than eighteen inches in diameter. They may be split while on the ground but it is generally easier to set short billets on end and drive the ax in the middle of the section, or between the center of the log and the bark. For billets no more than a foot in diameter the ax may be driven directly through the center.

Knots or the stubs of cut-off limbs can create a problem in splitting long or short logs. If possible the split should be planned to go directly through the center of the stub as well as the center of the log.

Only experience will make a man into a good axman, qualified to fell and buck and split with one primitive tool. Even the best of axmen, however, will resort to the use of wedges for splitting such long objects as fence rails, cabin sills and fence posts. Wedges, either of iron or wood, offer much better control than an ax, especially for one man working alone and wedging requires less energy.

Of course, all wedges require a concomitant striking tool: a steel sledge or go-devil for iron wedges and a wooden maul or mallet for wooden wedges known as gluts. The sledge should never be used on gluts, as its weight and hardness will soon splinter the wood. Wooden mauls and mallets should never be used on iron wedges, as the iron again splinters the wood in a short time.

A single-bit ax should never, under any circumstances, be used for wedge or sledge. Modern axes, made of steel throughout, will almost always crack across the eye when pounded on the poll or when the poll is used as a hammer face. Old-fashioned axes with soft iron body and steel bit welded to the iron will buckle at the eye when misused. Axes are for cutting only.

Wedges of iron and sledgehammers were furnished by the blacksmith in olden times and by hardware stores after 1860. Gluts, mauls and mallets, however, have almost invariably been homemade during the history of the frontier and have usually been preferred in backwoods areas. Often they are improvised from any available hardwood sapling in the woods by shaping

Splitting a knot   Glut with ring

with an ax. Often these very effective improvisations are discarded after the job of splitting rails or posts is finished. But
many backwoods men in the old days made permanent gluts
by carefully choosing a straight dogwood or ironwood (hornbeam) sapling, about 3½ inches in diameter, shaping its end
and shrinking a welded iron band around its butt in the same
manner as the band on a wagon wheel hub. Usually such gluts
are from fifteen to eighteen inches long. The angle of the wedge
is generally about 25°, slightly more sharply tapered than the
30° angle generally found in iron wedges, the narrower taper
allowing the glut to be pounded in more easily. After shaping,
the edge is usually trimmed with the ax so that it is about a
quarter inch wide, as opposed to the sharp edge found on
wedges. The final step in making a glut is to trim off the bark
for two or three inches from the butt as nearly round as possible
and then shrinking the band on. Such a glut, made from a good
piece of wood, can conceivably last a lifetime, if pounded only
with wooden striking tools.

    While simple to make and use, gluts were important tools
on the frontier. Seventeenth and eighteenth century colonists in

America were frequently advised to include several small iron bands in the equipment they brought from the mother country so that they could easily make wedges of wood.

Mauls required a little more effort to make and did not last as long as gluts, but the method of shaping was well within the talents of the average frontiersman and farmer and one may easily be shaped with only an ax if no other tools are available.

Just about any type of hardwood is suitable for a maul, but dogwood, elm, ironwood, hickory or beech is preferred, especially dogwood. To make a maul a sapling about six inches in diameter at a point three inches above the ground is felled by cutting the roots so that the root section, tough and almost impossible to split, may be incorporated into the head of the maul. A dogwood tree is quite easy to fell in this manner as it has no tap root to be severed; once the radial roots are cut the tree may be literally lifted out of its bed with little effort.

After felling, the trunk is cut off about forty inches from the ground point and all roots trimmed off even with the bole. From this portion the maul can be made with ax and knife alone, or more easily with saw, ax and drawknife. The object is, of course, to reduce the diameter of the upper thirty inches of the bole to the proper size for a comfortable handle, leaving the tough root section in its original dimension to serve as a head.

Using a saw, the bole is sawed into about 1½ to 2 inches all around at a point ten to twelve inches from the large end. All wood between this saw cut and the upper end is then removed, leaving a two-inch core about thirty inches long. This is carefully reduced with the ax to the proper diameter to fit the user's hands comfortably. Then it is dressed with knife or drawknife to the smoothness of an ax handle.

A railsplitter soon learns that using a maul with a handle longer than a maximum of thirty inches is extremely uncomfortable. Longer handles vibrate each time the maul makes contact with the glut, singing like a loose guitar string and badly stinging the hands.

It is necessary to use an ax or go-devil to start a glut in a log of any size. A split is started at the small end of the log and the glut inserted in the split and pounded in with the maul. When the glut is in as far as it will go another glut is inserted

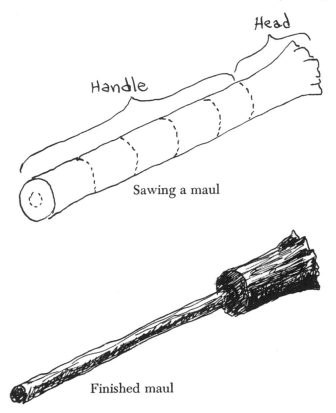

Sawing a maul

Finished maul

in the end of the split and pounded in, eventually loosening the first so that it may again be used in the end of the prolonged split.

Possibly one of the most exasperating experiences which can happen is for a splitter to insert the glut and pound it with all his might only to see the obstinate bit of banded wood bounce out of the split like a rubber ball, sometimes repeatedly. Two solutions are open for this problem: the glut can be placed in a wider part of the split or the glut can be shaped to a sharper taper. Modifying the taper is the most reliable of the two solutions, but the correction must be done with care and the taper shaped evenly so that the wood is not weakened to the extent that it will break, which is even more exasperating than having it bounce.

There are numbers of articles used in the backwoods which require split wood in one form or another but which are not usually included in the category of woodworking. Among these are withes, of hickory, oak or ash, used for tying, and then there are splint baskets of the same and other flexible woods. The technique of making these simple items is included here to clarify the techniques of splitting shingles and clapboards with a froe.

Withes, usually made of hickory, are no more than the half or quarter sections of slim hickory saplings, about an inch in diameter at the ground and about six feet long. Starting at the top of the sapling one splits the stem carefully through the dark pith line for about a foot. Then the knife is set aside, the legs of the split are grasped with the fingers of both hands with the heels of the hands together around the stem. The split is pulled slowly open by equal force from both hands as the heels slide down the stem.

Seldom does the split stay in the center of the stem for long, regardless of how even the pull of the fingers. One side will invariaby begin to run away from the center, and this must be watched for with great attention. When the split begins to run to one side the hand holding that side is kept stationary while the opposite half is pulled gently with the heel of the other hand, sliding downward so that it rests just below the end of the split. This will pull the split back to center when the heels of the hands are again placed together until the split begins to run out again. If the stem is large enough each half may be split again down the center using the same technique.

Basket splints are made essentially by the same method. A basket tree, however, should be from four to five inches in diameter at the base and from four to eight feet long depending on the size and type of basket to be made.

A sapling of this size is split into eighths, first through the center with the ax, starting at the top end. From then on the split is started with the ax for about eighteen inches, then the section is held on the ground by placing one's foot on it and the split is continued by pulling with both hands. If, under these circumstances, the split begins running out the section is reversed so that the thick side of the split is uppermost. Then the

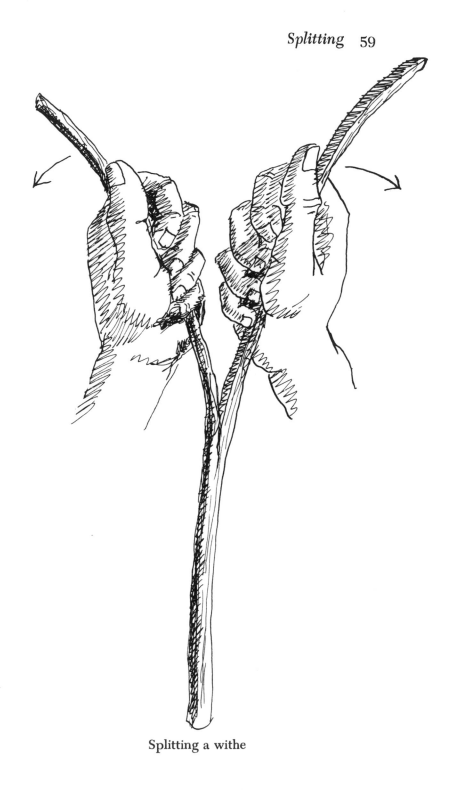

Splitting a withe

foot is placed on the section just below the end of the split and the upper leg is pulled gently but firmly until the split is again centered.

When sections have been reduced to a size which can be split with the hands the same technique as that used to split withes is applied.

Before the final splints are produced the bark and heartwood are removed with a knife. When sections have been reduced to a size which can be split with the hands the same technique as that used to split withes is applied. The split should be tangential to the annual rings.

Splints, if desired, may be smoothed by scraping with a knife. To finish, the rough splint is placed across the thigh of a seated person, the knife is held tightly athwart the splint and the splint is pulled under the knife edge enough times to remove all irregularities.

Essentially this basic technique of splitting is used in making shingles, shakes and clapboards. The difference is in the size of the wood being split and the use of the simple tools needed for riving boards of any type. Also there is considerable preparatory work needed on a tree before it can be divided into boards.

Indeed, possibly the most important aspect of splitting boards is to pick the proper tree, of a variety that will hold up for years without rotting and of exceptionally straight grain. Many old timers also paid considerable attention to cutting a board tree at a time of year when the sap was down and at a time of month when the moon was dark, if circumstances permitted, saying that boards made from a tree felled under these conditions will last years longer without warping. The dark of the moon in February is generally considered the ideal time to cut timber for any use.

But a good board tree is a rare phenomenon, sometimes hard to find in the woods. Most backwoodsmen, who want a roof to last, will check trees — oak, chestnut, pine or cypress — while on hunting expeditions and mark in their minds the locations of straight-grained trunks which might not be needed for years. The signs are subtle and not always unmistakable, but there has to be a starting point.

First of all the tree should be at least two feet in diameter at a point two feet above the ground, straight and without limbs for about twenty feet up. Often, but not always, a large even fork in the top indicates good grain. The most reliable sign of good grain, however, is the bark. If the ridges of bark run straight from roots to fork generally one can depend on the grain being straight. Any doubt will call for a further test, sometimes resorted to, which consists of chopping a large slab from the living tree to provide x-ray diagnosis of its grain. No tree which has a hollow limb or a sign of hollowness at the base is even considered, for this frequently means that the core of the tree is hollow, making it useless for boards. At times the most expert boardmaker may find what he thinks is the perfect tree only to find some hidden defect when the tree is felled and bucked. Usually, however, the boardmaker's instincts, as well as his judgment, meet the test.

After felling, the board tree is bucked with crosscut saw into sections about twenty-four to thirty inches long for shingles, perhaps three to four feet for shakes and up to six or seven feet for clapboards. Then each section is split radially with ax or go-devil or wedge into billets which measure about four inches on the base of the triangular section of each, and four to five inches from base to top of the cross section. Brittle heartwood and perishable sapwood must be discarded to the firewood pile, for heartwood is too hard to drive a shingle nail through, and sapwood will rot away within a year. On pine, cypress or chest-

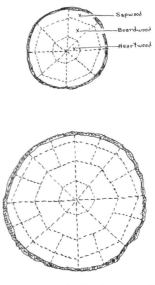

Suitable and unsuitable board trees as shown by bark

Splitting bolts from small and large board tree

nut there is no heartwood or sapwood; for these trees only the point of each section and the bark are discarded. Cedar needs have only the bark removed.

Of course, the size of the tree determines the number of billets per bucked section. A tree only two feet in diameter will yield only a single circle of billets after heartwood and sapwood have been removed. A log three to four feet in diameter might have two circles of usable billets. Split boards are not required to match any predetermined width and variation in the size of billets is unimportant.

Once billets are prepared the special, peculiar tools of riving are employed, the froe, the short maul and the brake, which is usually referred to in the backwoods simply as the fork. Like most hand tools, all these are ancient in origin.

The froe is no more than a piece of wrought iron half an inch thick, two inches wide and eighteen to twenty inches long, doubled back upon itself and forge welded to form a round eye about two inches in diameter. One side of this instrument is drawn out to a blunt knife-edge and a rough handle, eighteen inches long, of hickory, dogwood, ash or whatever, is inserted in the eye, extending out of the eye on the side opposite the edge.

Brakes for riving are usually prepared on the spot from an acute fork found in the top of the felled board tree, or from any

Froe

Froe, maul and brake in use

convenient tree nearby. Its base, at the fork, is at least eight inches in diameter while the legs of the fork are from four to six inches in diameter and from four to six feet long. This is leaned against a stump or tree and staked securely to the ground with one leg rising above the other, the plane of the two forks being at about a 30° angle from the ground. In function the fork simulates the heels of the hands while splitting withes or splints.

Sometimes a suitable fork is unavailable and a brake must be improvised. The boardmaker might stake a small six-inch log to the ground about six inches in front of a two-foot log, each of the logs replacing the legs of the fork. At other times he might find two roots juxtaposed in the same relation as the legs of the desired fork and use these as his brake.

Actual riving, for shingles, shakes or clapboards, is simple, employing the same principle as splitting withes, but sometimes difficult in technique and requiring the same basic instincts and experience needed in other handicrafts. An important, indeed essential, bit of foreknowledge is which of three methods of splitting should be applied to the variety of board tree being split.

Cedar wood, either the red aromatic cedar found in the East or the white, light cedar of the Northwest coast, may be split in any direction without first having to split a log section into billets. The log itself is squared with froe and maul and the resulting square section is split down the middle. Each half is then split again down the middle and the process is continued until the entire section has been split to the desired thickness for shingles or boards.

Before the white man appeared, the Haida, Tlingit, Kwakiutl and other aboriginal tribes of the Northwest coast constructed sizable houses of large boards split from the fallen trunks of the huge cedars found in that area. Having no metal suitable for making froes they used a most ingenious method to split out large boards with bone and wooden wedges and wooden mauls.

First they cut two notches on the trunk of a fallen cedar, the distance between the notches being equal to the desired length of the intended board. Each notch was cut to a depth of about two inches, equal to the desired thickness of the board. Then they drove in a series of wedges between the bottom points

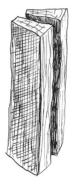
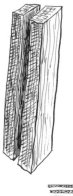

| Splitting bark from cedar | Diagram of splitting radially | Diagram of bastard splitting |

of the two notches and split off a board. After the board had been split off two more notches were cut and the process repeated.

Oak, pine, chestnut and cypress all must have the billets split radially, as already described, but once the billets are prepared they are split differently in oak or poplar from the method used for pine, cypress and chestnut.

For oak, generally white or chestnut oak, shingles are split radially, or with what is called a regular split. Consequently, oak shingles are slightly thicker on one edge than on the other. This inequality, of course was most suitable for overlapping clapboards which were always split from oak.

The third method is called bastard splitting by the people of the Smoky Mountains, where shingles are still being made by hand in the 1970s. It is used on pine, cypress and chestnut, the use of the latter now of long lamented memory.

The derivation of the term *bastard* in respect to splitting wood is unknown and possibly will never be known. It means merely that the billets split radially from a section of log are split tangentially to the annual rings to divide into boards. As opposed to cedar and oak boards, those of pine and chestnut and cypress split from one billet are of even thickness throughout, but of varying widths. If these woods are split like oak they will lack strength and will split again when being nailed to the purlins, the poles or boards fastened horizontally to roof beams. And, while not split with froe and maul, fence palings and tobacco sticks of pine were always split bastard fashion with an ax and afterward split to proper width.

Regardless of whether or not boards are split by regular or bastard method, however, the use of froe and maul and brake is the same. The billet is stood on its end and the froe placed as nearly as possible in the exact middle of the end. It is then hammered into the grain, causing the billet to yield two smaller billets of two inch thickness. Usually the original billet is thick enough so that it does not matter too much if the split runs out to one side a little, and the bulk of the original billet usually keeps the split straight. It is in the halving of these smaller billets that the science and instincts of the boardmaker and design of froe and brake are all employed to change the process of splitting into riving, wherein the even quality of the boards is determined.

Again the froe is placed as nearly in the middle of the billet as possible and pounded with the maul to start the split. As long as the split stays in the middle of the billet all is well and no riving skill need be called upon. But if the split does begin to run toward one side, the billet is placed in the brake with the thick side of the split down resting on the higher leg of the brake at the end of the split, the bottom end of the billet being held by the bottom leg of the brake.

At this point the handle of the froe is rotated downward, opening the split so that a hand can be placed in it to press downward on the side of the billet below the split. While pressing with one hand the froe handle is rotated slightly, but not enough to allow the split to close, and the froe blade is pushed downward to lengthen the split a fraction at a time. If, as sometimes happens, the split begins to run out in the opposite direction the billet is removed from the brake and reversed so that the thick side again rests on the higher leg of the brake.

In riving the higher leg of the brake serves the same function as the heel of the hand board, and the inserted hand serves as fingers in the simple splitting of withes. The inexperienced boardmaker can learn much about the principle of riving if he splits a few withes before attempting boards.

By now the original billet has been split once and riven once, the end result being two boards about an inch thick on the thick edge, if of oak, or an even thickness of one inch if of cedar, pine, chestnut or cypress. These must be halved once again by riving to produce two shingles each. The same method of inserting the hand and wiggling the froe while the board is held in the brake is followed. There is more chance of the split running out in riving a board only one inch thick, but this problem is compensated for by the greater ease of correcting the run-out on thinner stuff.

Making shingles two feet long or clapboards six feet long uses exactly the same tools and same principles but a slight difference in technique because of the longer, more awkward length of the clapboards.

The sections from which clapboards are rived are split out of the log with maul and glut to a thickness of about two inches on the thick edge. Sapwood and heartwood are discarded as with shingle billets. From then on the froe and brake are employed with some slight differences. For one, the brake is staked so that the legs of the fork are almost on the same level in order to allow the much longer board to be drawn between the legs for its whole length. And since the boardmaker cannot stand the six-foot section on end he leans it against the brake with one end pushed against a tree or a stake and drives the froe in obliquely to the ground.

Riving clapboards is done exactly as riving shingles with one hand pressing downward the bottom leg of the split, the froe being wiggled downward to lengthen the split and the board being reversed inside the fork to remedy run-outs.

Clapboards can be rived without a fork if the billet is first split with froe and maul for about eighteen inches. At this point the long billet may be secured on the ground by holding it with one foot, while the started split is pulled upward. If the split begins to run out the billet is reversed and the opposite side pulled upward.

For obvious reasons the trees used for clapboards were more carefully picked even than those for shingles. It is doubtful that any clapboards have been riven anywhere since about 1850.

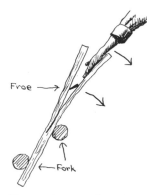

Correcting a split which
begins to run out

Splitting clapboards on the ground

Once one rives a few shingles he will see the advantage of a natural uncut tree fork over improvised brakes; the board being rived in the fork can be moved laterally to keep the end of the split positioned over the top leg of the fork without losing the hold of the bottom leg against the bottom of the board.

It is considered preferable to install split shingles while the wood is green, for this minimizes the unwanted splitting from nailing which is likely to occur when seasoned shingles are nailed down. On the other hand no sensible man is apt to waste a good, straight-grained board tree even if he cannot use all the shingles he produces. So excess shingles may be stacked flat in piles which have the grain of alternate layers running perpendicular to each other. Generally the stacks are made up to five feet tall, under a roof, and a heavy section of log or a couple of flat stones placed on top to weigh down the shingles and keep them flat.

Most backwoodsmen preferred to lay shingles as they came from the brake, claiming that the rough and beautiful texture of the split fibers will channel rainwater more effectively than a smooth surface. In the towns, however, there was often a preference for dressed shingles. How this was accomplished easily and quickly will be described in a later chapter.

Wooden shingles are not available in many lumber yards

today because they constitute a fire hazard and are much more expensive to make and install than asphalt roofing. Hand split shingles of quality are practically impossible to find unless one first finds one of the few remaining boardmakers who still lives in some of the backwoods areas of the nation, or unless one wishes to do it himself in true pioneer tradition.

Perhaps the extra leisure time expected of our future will encourage the self-training of a new generation of splitters. And whether one makes rails with ax and glut or makes boards with more sophisticated froe and fork, splitting a log into smaller objects is satisfying to some obscure primitive instinct and at times requires more intellect than might be imagined.

CHAPTER III

The Workbench

No TOOL in the woodworker's shop is more important than the bench. It's not a cutting, boring, hewing, sawing, scraping, carving tool, but the evolution of these categories to a status of eloquence was largely because of the presence and evolution of the bench. It's not a hand tool, but most of the hand tools used by carpenter or joiner can be operated more precisely, and certainly more comfortably, because of it.

The bench is a body tool, a holding tool, a basic tool. It must be always looked upon as a tool, and used as such.

With all its many auxiliary parts, attached or detached, the bench gives the worker a thousand extra hands without which the Chippendales and Adamses and Goddards might never have reached their eminence in the waning days of woodworking by hand. And, although many other factors must be considered, it is interesting to speculate that few cabinetmakers are known by name before the development of the bench to its final form in the last years of the eighteenth and early years of the nineteenth centuries, the years when the best of our woodworkers lived. An efficient bench not only allows the artist to do better work but it also increases his production without lowering his standards of design and construction.

Ideally the bench itself must go far beyond the low crude benches first devised by Roman woodworkers to provide an even surface upon which to smooth a plank with the newly invented plane. Its smooth, level top is still essential but it should be six feet or more in length and of a height which strikes the standing worker about midway between his wrists and elbows when his arms are hanging at his side. This allows him to push plane, saw, chisel, all without stooping and without strain. Each worker in a shop should have his own personal bench, as was the case in the finer cabinet shops before the industrial age, or each worker should adjust another's bench by sawing or elevating it to fit his own body and standards of comfort.

Possibly the earliest attachment to the bench was the stop designed to hold a board while it is being planed. Originally a wooden peg was used for the stop and later a short iron rod with a triangular head, its base having teeth cut into it, and bent upward, with the apex of the triangle bent downward to bite into the bench top.

The stop is held in place by inserting its shank into one of a series of small holes bored into the bench top. Usually two stops are used to hold the end of the board and two or three along the side of the board opposite the position of the planer.

After 1800 a wooden stop was generally readopted. This modern form consisted of a small peg an inch square, offset on each side to form a shank three quarters of an inch square with a one inch head, the head being three eighths of an inch deep. Frequently a small nail pierced the head midway in its depth so that the point protruded an eighth of an inch to substitute for the teeth on the head of the earlier type iron stop. Wooden stops may be used in exactly the same manner as the metal ones. They were adopted mainly because they were more suitable for use with the end vise of the improved type workbench which generally appeared in America and England at the same time, around 1800.

But stops cannot be used to hold a board on one edge while its other edge is being planed. For this purpose both top and front bench clamps were invented at some unknown date. Both types functioned on the principle of jambing, but the forms of the two are somewhat different.

A top bench clamp in its earliest form is no more than a flat piece of plank about three quarters of an inch thick, four inches wide and six to eight inches long. In one end is sawn an acute V-shaped notch, usually about 30°. This board is nailed securely to the top of the bench at one end toward the front, the notch

Early bench showing height

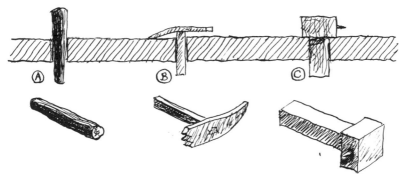

Bench stops in place and out. Peg—iron—wood

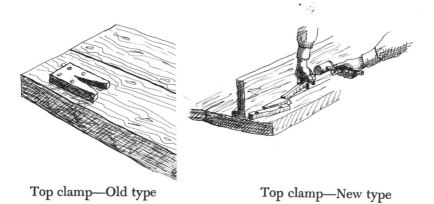

Top clamp—Old type   Top clamp—New type

pointing toward the other end. To use, the planer sets the end of a board on edge into the notch and jambs it tightly by tapping; it is removed easily by a couple of taps on the jambed end.

This simple clamp was improved in the eighteenth or early nineteenth century by constructing it of two narrow boards which were nailed or screwed to the bench top in a V-shape with two wedges which fit between the legs of the V. The board to be planed is set on edge between the legs of the V and wedges are tapped in on each side to clamp it tightly. There is a bevel on the inside of the V boards fitting bevels on the outside of the wedges so that the wedges are locked to prevent their rising upward when tapped in tightly. The old and the new type makes a most efficient clamp, absolutely essential to the joiner before the screw vise first appeared around the second half of the seventeenth century. Top clamps are still a handy device for any woodworking bench.

Early Continental joiners used a similar device fixed to the front of the bench top, although for some reason it was never adopted by English joiners. It consists of half of a natural, or simulated, tree fork, screwed or pegged to the front of the bench so that the end of a board being planed can be jambed between the leg of the fork and the edge of the bench top. The length of the board is supported by pegs which fit into holes in the bench

Side clamp showing supporting pegs

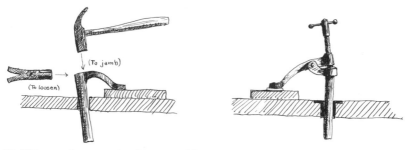

Holdfast—showing jambing and loosening   Modern holdfast

legs, each leg having a series of holes to fit various widths of board. This type of front clamp was entirely supplanted by the front vise, but supporting pegs in holes were retained when the vise was adopted.

There is another quite ingenious and efficient holding tool which probably originated in Roman times and has now been consigned to virtual oblivion for some unknown reason. It is called a holdfast and in function it quite confirms its name. Basically it is no more than a square or round bar of iron fifteen inches long, flattened for about six inches on one end, the flattened end being bent roughly to a right angle. It resembles an inverted L with the leg curved slightly downward. A holdfast is used by inserting its shank into a hole, only slightly larger than the shank, bored through the bench top. Any stuff being held is placed on the bench top under the tip of the leg and the shank is hammered downward, jambing it into the hole. To avoid scarring the board being held, a small piece of thin, soft wood should be placed between the work and the tip of the holdfast.

It is quite amazing to the uninitiated how tightly this ancient tool holds work to the bench top. It is easily dislodged by tapping the shank at its top opposite the leg until it is unjambed and may be lifted from the hole.

A more modern version of the holdfast with a pivoting leg tightened by a thumbscrew is available from a limited number of woodworking supply houses. The modern type, however, is no more efficient than the ancient.

Another ancient auxiliary bench tool, seldom identified when found in antique shops, is the side rest, sometimes called a saw rest. Like the holdfast it has virtually disappeared from

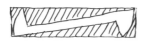

Side rest—By itself and in use

modern workshops in America, though still used in Europe, but it has wide application in any home or professional woodworking shop regardless of the degree of mechanization. Perhaps its simplicity seems to deny its identity and usefulness. It is no more than a foot-long board some three to four inches wide and about as thick, sawn to form shoulders at each end, the shoulders being on opposite sides and the connecting portion. When the side rest is placed upon the bench top one shoulder catches on the front of the bench, the other pointing upward. To saw a small board or piece of molding the worker holds the stuff tightly against the upper shoulder, pressing forward to keep the lower shoulder tight against the bench front, and easily saws his stuff in two without having to resort to holdfast or vise. The thickness of the connecting wood between the shoulders forms a shelf which keeps the stuff off the bench top and prevents scarring the top with the saw.

Some side rests were as much as a foot wide to support long boards better. Most frequently the worker would use two rests, adjusting the distance between them to suit his work. Side rests can easily be improvised by nailing shoulders on the ends of a two-by-four, but the rests shaped by saw are preferred by the true professional.

Every woodworker of modern times is familiar with the wood vise as an essential extra pair of hands with more power than any human hands. Modern vises, mass produced of metal with steel screws and guides and provisions for facing the metal jaws with wood, operate on exactly the same principle and perform the same function as the front vises of joiners' benches in the seventeenth century. Superficial design and the basic materials used are the only real differences between the old and the new, but these differences necessitated slightly different techniques in use.

Old vises come in two forms, one with a horizontal front jaw and one with a vertical jaw. Both types are closed with beautiful wooden screws usually from 2–2½ inches in diameter. Early horizontal vises often had two screws, one at each end of the jaw. The stuff to be worked is placed between the front jaw and the front of the bench, which serves as the back jaw, and one screw is tightened first, then the other. Later horizontal vises, the improved type which appeared around 1800 and which served as the prototype for the modern vise made of steel, have one central screw and wooden guide bar at each end which keep the front jaw parallel to the bench top as the screw is tightened, exactly as with a modern vise.

Vises with vertical jaws, which generally follow the form of the ancient blacksmith's leg vise and which may be the oldest form of the wood vise, are made differently and operate differently. They are mounted in front of one of the legs of the bench, for one difference, or in front of a thick vertical board

Improvised side rest

Horizontal wood vise

Horizontal vise with guides

which is inset into the bench top with its top surface cut off even with the top. A joiner's vise has its top even with the top of the bench while a wheelwright's wood vise has its top protruding above the bench top as with metalworkers' vises.

The screw is usually about a foot from the top of the vise. It passes through the front jaw, being prevented from going all the way by a turned boss which is pierced for a wooden handle with a knob at each end. The screw is held in place by what is called a garter, a small piece of wood set in a mortise which engages in a shallow groove turned in the screw. Not only does the garter fix the screw in place but it also makes the front jaw move backward as the screw is turned to disengage the jaws. Of course, the screw also pierces the vertical board of the back jaw where it goes through a large wooden nut which is socketed or glued to the back to the back jaw.

Unlike the blacksmith's leg vise, with a pivoting jaw, the vertical wood vise must have its jaws parallel. This is accomplished by mortising a small board of a strong wood, 2 x 2 inches, into the front jaw a foot from its lower end, to serve as a guide. The guide is pierced by holes every inch or so along its length, and it is inserted through a matching hole in the back jaw.

Vertical wood vise

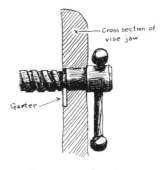

Garter mechanism

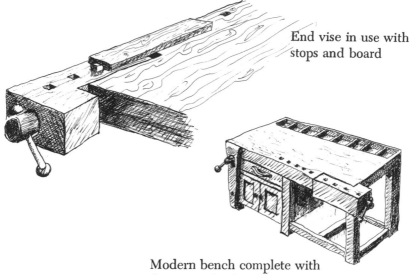

End vise in use with
stops and board

Modern bench complete with
drawer and cabinet

As the screw is tightened the guide moves on its appointed way through the back jaw, and when the vise tightens on its piece of work a small peg, hanging conveniently by a cord attached to the back jaw, is inserted in the appropriate hole in the guide. This peg, ½ inch in diameter and of wood or iron, serves to keep the jaws nearly parallel and therefore more efficient.

Vises made entirely of wood, although seeming somewhat awkward, must be judged in the context of their times. Being all wood each could be repaired in the woodworking shop by the woodworker. Indeed, such a vise could be made entirely by the woodworker, an important factor in the days before mass production.

After about 1800, and continuing in America until at least World War I, the bench of the hand craftsman in wood was also equipped with an end vise in addition to the front vise. The end vise has a peculiarly L-shaped jaw which fits into the corner of the bench opposite the front vise, on the worker's right hand. It is horizontal and heavy and, like its brother, actuated by a wooden screw. On the front, long side, of the jaw it has one or two square holes into which stops are inserted and the bench top has up to eight or ten such holes in a line parallel to the front edge of the bench, also intended for the insertion of stops. Boards being planed or carved or bored are laid flat between a stop in the vise and a stop in the bench top and clamped tightly while being worked, thereby abolishing the need for the holdfast and for more than two stops. The short leg which bends around the corner can be utilized as an extra vise for short pieces. The end vise is also known as a screwbox.

Such are the major components and auxiliaries of the joiner's workbench. While these were standard during the evolution of the bench from ancient times until the age of machines, during the times when a woodworker made his own bench, a number of variations in design might be found.

Some craftsmen in wood prepared a depressed shallow shelf with dividers across the back of the bench to hold tools while work was being done and this feature has been incorporated in the design of some of the fine workbenches still being made and sold by European tool factories. At other times workers have demurred at altering the pristine condition of the top with holes and mortises for stops and holdfasts and have nailed or screwed a replaceable board pierced to receive these appendages, on the front of the bench.

And while early workbenches, before the seventeenth century, often had the legs merely mortised into the heavy top without stretchers, later benches did employ stretchers between the legs. Often the stretchers were used to support a shelf for storing planks and scraps. This practice had the advantage of adding weight to the bench, stabilizing it all the more. Many later benches had the underside enclosed and partitioned for cabinets, frequently with drawers added for tool storage, all of which added convenience and efficiency to the use of the bench itself as a tool.

Also there were special benches, especially in large shops, where special work such as sawing or cutting veneer was done. These had to be placed properly within the shop. For instance, a bench on which long planks were bucked might be placed near a door or window to allow the length of the plank to project beyond the limits of the shop.

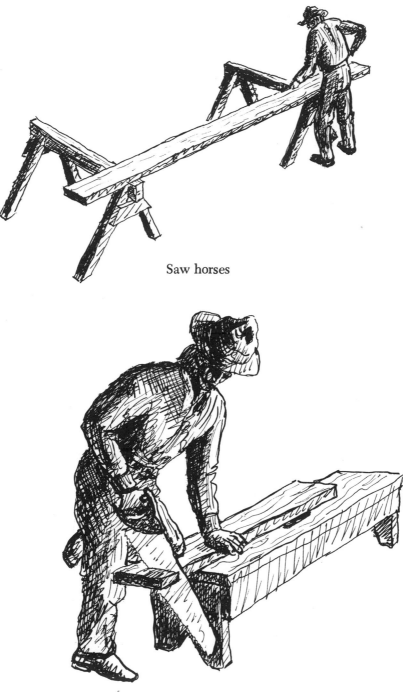

Saw horses

Sawing bench showing height

The regular bench, however, was usually placed against a wall to provide a maximum of working space in the shop and to allow the worker to reach wall shelves on which tools were kept.

Such items as saw horses and small sawing benches were important adjuncts to the main bench and were found in olden times, as today, in almost every shop. Before nails became available cheap saw horses were generally made by mortising four splayed legs into a heavy plank or puncheon. Later in the days of plentiful sawmills and wire nails saw horses were, and still are, made of a two by four with legs of the same material nailed to the rail and braced at each end with a piece of scrap lumber. Saw horses of the nailed variety are considered quite expendable items and usually end in the scrap pile after limited use.

Not so with the small sawing benches which are still preferred by some workers. These are made like a short sitting bench with a 1 x 12-inch board, or two smaller boards, for a top, two legs of the same material and a wide rail nailed to the legs at each side. The legs almost always have an angle cut from the bottom of each to provide four supporting surfaces which give considerably more stability than two broad legs. Sawing benches are as high as the knees of the worker, enabling him to secure comfortably with one knee a board being sawed, without undue strain on back or shoulders. Usually the sawing bench is about two feet long. Often the craftsman will cut a hand hole in the top board so that the bench may be picked up and moved with one hand.

A well-planned shop centers around the workbench. And while the shop space itself dictates the location of every piece of equipment the ideal arrangement is to place lathe and treadle jig saw, tool storage racks and lumber supply where they can be conveniently reached from a position in front of the bench and from where work done can be returned to the bench with a minimum of effort.

When planning a shop of the old style, one should build or acquire the workbench first. Then, in the spirit of the golden age of hand craftsmanship, he can make all the wooden components of most of the tools he may need for a lifetime of carpentry and cabinetmaking and satisfying pleasure.

CHAPTER IV

Sawing

IN ALL the years since the saw was invented during the Stone Age the principles of sawing wood have changed hardly at all. The forms of saws have changed, and form dictates some minor changes in techniques and handling, but only to keep the saw blade in its proper position and move it in its proper rhythm with comfort and stamina. The principles of sawing are quite immutable, a fact understood when one closely examines saws and the design of saws.

A saw is no more than a long thin strip of steel which has triangular teeth formed into one edge. (Saws with teeth on both edges, of different fineness, are still used by Oriental carpenters, but Western saws have commonly been single-edged.) Each tooth is a small cutting instrument which performs inexorably in concert with its neighbors. Because the grain of wood has a different character when cut *across* the grain than when cut *with* the grain, different cutting edges are needed on wood saws. The crosscut saw has teeth filed to sharp points and edges which cut like small pointed knives through the successive layers of grain. Rip saws, however, those which partition a board lengthwise, have teeth filed like small chisels which dig rather than cut the kerf.

Both rip and crosscut saws have been made available in varying degrees of fineness probably since the saw was first made of steel. Fineness is designated by the number of teeth, or points, to the inch in smaller saws, and the number of points to a foot in large two-man saws.

81

Saws are also typed as push or pull, according to the direction in which they cut. Most hand saws used in the Western world are push saws and the teeth point forward so they may bite more deeply into the wood each time the saw is pushed through the kerf, the return stroke being only to reposition the saw for another push.

Certain saws, though, such as narrow-bladed framed turning saws, have always been pull saws because pulling eliminates the possibility of the narrow blade buckling when pushed through the kerf. As a consequence the teeth always point toward the worker.

Ancient saw

Teeth in crosscut saw

Teeth on rip saw

Pull saw and push saw

Before the making of steel became somewhat scientific with the invention of the Catalan furnace in the fourteenth century all hand saws were pull saws. Since the metal of that day was so unevenly carborized, and difficult to temper evenly buckling was a common occurrence when the blade was pushed. Oriental saws are generally pull saws, even in modern times; possibly because of the stronger influence of tradition in Eastern cultures.

Since metal expands from the heat of friction developed in sawing, a wood saw will bind and become immobile and useless unless the kerf is widened by slightly spreading alternate teeth in opposite directions. The spread of the teeth is called the set of the saw, and setting is essential in all but one or two special types of saws. Saw teeth need only be set at a very slight angle from the plane of the blade, but setting is a delicate operation since all teeth must have exactly the same set or the saw will become uncontrollable and inefficient. Setting is done by a saw set, in olden times no more than a bar with slots of varying width cut into its edge to accommodate varying thicknesses of saw blades. To use, the saw set is slid over a tooth and the tooth then levered outward to its desired set. Later saw sets were designed with a miniature anvil with an angled face and a pivoting jaw, also with an angled face which was tapped with a hammer to bend the tooth. Still later devices eliminated the hammer, but not the design principle, by using what is essentially a pair of pliers with angled faces on the jaws. Large two-man saws may be set with a small stake anvil, which may be driven into a stump or block of wood, and a light hammer.

Information about push and pull saws, the designation of fineness by points, the difference between rip and crosscut saws and the purpose of setting is extremely basic information which was seldom touched upon in older texts because it was taken for granted that any woodworker knew it in the days of hand-craftsmanship in wood. Conditions have changed since World War II, certainly in America more than anywhere else in the world. The American woodworker today, even the hobbyist, is so used to machine tools and finds the variety of hand tools available so relatively limited that he often has no understanding of the basic design of hand tools. When he goes to a hardware store to buy a saw he merely asks for a saw. If the saw

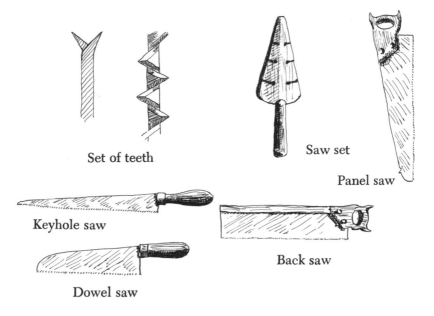

Set of teeth

Saw set

Panel saw

Keyhole saw

Back saw

Dowel saw

eventually ceases to cut efficiently he doesn't know why. Accordingly, he loses much of the sheer pleasure of using hand tools, or of putting a bit of himself into an article he makes. An understanding of hand tools is elemental to the enjoyment of handcraftsmanship, hence this somewhat detailed information on the terminology of using saws. It is an attempt to make this work more nearly of universal interest by filling in some knowledge which may not be otherwise available to newcomers in the field of working wood by hand.

The forms of saws used throughout the history of woodworking are legion, many of them known only because of archaeological investigation and many of them obviously deficient in design when compared with saws used since the beginning of the seventeenth century. A worker who understands the use of relatively later saws may consider himself well grounded in old ways of working wood.

Old saws came in two major forms, the framed saws and the unframed saws.

Among the unframed saws are two or three which still find limited use in modern woodworking. One of these is the two-man

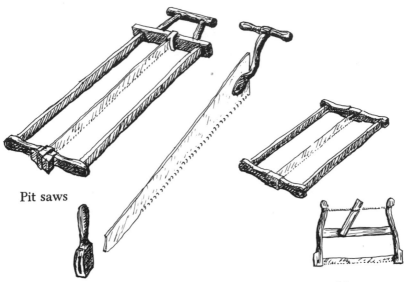

Pit saws

Frame saw and bow saw

crosscut used for sawing heavy timber. Others are the carpenter's hand saw, or panel saw, the keyhole saw for making curved kerfs, the dowel saw and several varieties of backsaws. Backsaws were used in a slightly modified form by ancient Roman woodworkers. The more modern types consist of an unframed rectangular blade stiffened by a sleeve of iron or brass along the back and furnished with either a straight-turned handle or a closed handle. Types of backsaws include the dovetail, the tenon and the miter saw. Pit saws in the latter part of the eighteenth century, after the introduction of cast steel, were also offered unframed.

Framed saws had two major forms, one known simply as a frame saw and the other with a different type frame known generally as a bow saw.

The frame saw was invariably for ripping and was designed so that the stretchers on the side of the frame would clear the edges of a board or log being ripped. Pit saws, veneer saws and felloe saws all came within this category as well as the framed panel saws which were in general use until the seventeenth century.

Bow saws, with one exception, were used for crosscutting. This type has a relatively narrow blade set in the end of two narrow boards roughly perpendicular to the blade. Midway between the boards is a stretcher and the ends of the boards are connected with a stout cord loop through which a short stick is inserted to twist the loop, spreading the opposite ends of the frame to tauten the saw blade. When the cord is twisted tightly one end of the short board is stopped by the stretcher to maintain the twist. This form of saw was used by carpenters as a crosscut saw until the appearance of the wide-bladed panel saw in the seventeenth century. It survived in the bucksaw, used by farmers in America for sawing firewood until World War II, and in the turning saw which disappeared in America around 1900 but is still generally used by European cabinetmakers. The turning saw has its blade filed for ripping but it is called upon to cross cut to some extent when cutting fretwork or other shapes in furniture.

Three modern modifications of metal framed saws are available at hardware stores or woodworking supply houses during the 1970s. The most common is the coping saw, frequently miscalled a jig saw. Rarely one sees a fretwork saw, very

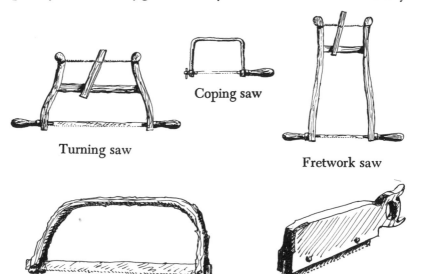

Coping saw

Turning saw

Fretwork saw

Ancient bow saw

Rabbet saw

similar to the coping saw but with a much deeper frame. Also common in hardware stores is the modern bow saw consisting of a bowed pipe with a crosscut saw blade stretched between its ends. While modern, the contemporary bow saw has exactly the same design as bow saws with wooden bows used in Slavic countries in ancient times.

A specialized saw, housed rather than framed, is the rabbet saw, used mostly by cabinetmakers over the centuries but employed occasionally by master carpenters in the building of stairs and built-in bookcases. It consists of a crosscut saw blade mounted in a block which has a closed handle behind and sometimes a horn before. Actually it is a saw blade in a plane stock.

Each of these many types of saw requires a slightly different technique to use in the most efficient manner.

Two-man crosscut saws were used by the ancient Egyptians, in an age of pull saws, and probably the technique of using this lumberman's saw was developed by the Egyptians and not changed since. Techniques for using the crosscut saw are described in the first chapter of this book since this ancient tool is used almost wholly in conjunction with the ax to fell and buck large trees.

Other two-man saws are the pit and the veneer saw, both of which are rip saws, but now obsolete in America and Western Europe. The veneer saw is a frame saw, large enough to require two men to hold it in position but actually being pulled by only one man while the other merely restores the blade to a pulling position since the chisel teeth point toward the sawyer. Material being sawn is clamped tightly in a large vise, the kerf going from top to bottom.

Pit saws are still used during the moon-landing age in the Orient, the Middle East, Africa and South America though gradually disappearing as these areas adopt the progressive attitudes and machinery of America and Europe. Logs to be sawn into boards are supported on two joists over a deep pit, hence the name, or more usually rest on a scaffold high enough for a man to stand beneath it while the sawyer stands above on the log itself. The cut is made on the downward stroke so that gravity can help pull, and the ripping teeth point downward.

Until the later years of the eighteenth century pit saws were all framed. After the invention of cast steel, however, these saws were made as merely a long tapered blade with an attached horizontal handle with iron shank at the butt of the wedge, called a tiller handle and an easily removable handle of wood, which slipped over the point of the wedge and jambed there, on the lower end.

Logs, or balks, to be pit sawn required some preparation. Usually the bark was removed and a straight line marked on the upper surface with a chalk or charcoal line. Sometimes they were hewn flat on two sides before sawing, sometimes not. After preparation the logs were raised and placed on the trestle or, before the end of the seventeenth century, over the pit.

There is some variation in the form of trestles. Most, in countries all over the world, seem to have always been made of a cross beam on which one end of the log is tied or dogged with metal dogs similar to a huge, flat staple. The other end is then supported on what is called a crutch, a light vertical support with two legs and shoulders on which the log rests.

At shipyards or regular lumber yards before the eighteenth century the crutch was not used, the timber being supported on two heavy beams. No doubt this more permanent trestle was more practical only when there were enough laborers around to manhandle the heavy timbers as needed to reposition the log when the saw reached a crossbeam.

In a few areas the log was laid on one lengthwise slanting beam which rested on a trestle or post. With this method the log being sawn had one end chained to a ground anchor so that the end being sawn was cantilevered over the end of the supporting beam.

Sawing commences on the end supported by the crutch which is set some three or four feet from the end. To start, the sawyer, standing on the balk, makes short strokes with the saw to begin the kerf along the chalk line, the lower man only supporting and guiding the saw to assure that the plane of the blade is perpendicular to the ground. Once the kerf is begun the sawyer raises his end of the tool to shoulder height and then pushes it downward, the weight of the saw doing most of the work, while the lower man guides. For the return stroke the pitman

Pit sawing

Pit sawing trestle with crutch

lifts the blade while the sawyer guides it so that its teeth remain on the chalk line.

When the saw reaches the crutch, or first cross beam, it is removed and the next cut started. When all the boards in a balk are started for about three feet the saw is removed and the crutch moved so that the balk is supported with its extreme end resting on the shoulders of the crutch.

Now to finish each of the cuts to the end of the balk. The saw blade must be disengaged from frame or handle and inserted into one of the kerfs behind the relocated crutch. With frame saws the wedge which tautens the blade must be knocked out, the blade disengaged from the pin which fastens it to the ring in which the wedge is inserted and then reinserted through a kerf, whereupon the blade is pinned once more and the ring wedged to tauten the blade. After this sawing recommences.

The process is much easier with an unframed pit saw. Here the wooden handle on the small end of the blade is unjambed and slipped off and the blade reinserted in a kerf. In a second or so the wooden handle can be replaced and sawing recommenced with a minimum of time.

A slightly different technique, easier in some ways, is employed on trestles with one beam on which the balk is secured lengthwise. On this type trestle all kerfs are cut to the end of the beam and then the balk is moved forward several feet and sawing continued without the need to disengage blade or handle.

In most cases the kerfs, regardless of the type trestle, are cut only to about six inches from the end, where it rests on the beam. At this point the balk is removed and the boards are separated by sawing them from the butt of the balk with a cross-cut saw.

A minor piece of equipment for pit sawing is the wide-brimmed hat worn by the pitman to keep sawdust from going down the neck of his shirt.

There are some advantages to using the large two-man saws, as compared to smaller saws, to achieve accuracy and straightness in the kerf. For one thing two men can exercise greater control over the saw; for another the width of a large saw blade serves to guide the cutting. Also the very weight of a two-man saw serves to set the teeth more firmly into the wood while the coarseness of the teeth and length of blade enable the tool to cut as much as an inch with each stroke. None of these advantages adheres to smaller saws. With them it is a case of man against material, man's eye guiding, a good right arm making up for lack of weight and cultivated patience substituting for coarseness of teeth.

All, however, was not toil and trouble when using the framed handsaws before the advent of the unframed panel saw. Old carpenters who had nothing but a primitive bow saw and much patience must have frequently been frustrated in their attempts to saw a straight line, which is the objective of using all saws except those designed to saw a crooked line. But the framed crosscut saws — with substantial posts and stretchers, the blade tautened efficiently with a twisted cord — offered certain, but not overwhelming advantages over the later, still modern panel saws. For one, framed crosscut saws can be grasped with two hands which provide good control on the route of each rhythmic stroke. Of course, the stuff being sawed with two hands must be secured in a vise or crosslegged saw horse, or with a holdfast or a clamp or a dependable apprentice.

Grasp on bow saw showing
line of blade before shoulder

As with later hand saws, in starting the framed crosscut is held so that its blade makes about a 45° angle with the top of the board to be cut, and the kerf is started on the corner of the stuff.

If the corner catches in between two teeth, however, it tends to cam the saw blade upward on either a pushing or a pulling stroke, causing it to leap from the proposed course of the kerf and damage the corner of the stuff, or a thumb, in a spot where damage is not desired. To avoid this the workman grasps the frame of the saw with his right hand directly above the blade, the line of the blade being directly in front of his right shoulder. The left hand grabs the post of the frame above the right hand, the left arm passing across the chest. Then the blade is laid on the corner, angled properly, two or three teeth from the end nearest the right hand. Without any downward pressure, other than from the weight of the saw, the workman gently draws the saw toward himself so that the back side of the teeth perform a rasping effect on the wood. When the end of the blade is reached, the saw is raised and the gentle pulling is repeated until a channel, long enough at its bottom to support three or four points, is cut. This channel, now probably deep enough although the type and character of the wood calls for some judgment on the matter, will serve as a guide for the blade so it may be pushed to commence the penetrating cut for which it is designed. From this point until the stuff is cut through the workman pulls and pushes the saw evenly and rhythmically, generally holding the blade at its original 45° angle to the stuff, but changing the angle temporarily if the kerf deviates from the line to be cut. In case of deviation the blade is held at about a 10° angle to the top of the stuff and sawing continues to create a new, shallow channel along the cut line. Once the deviation is corrected the blade is returned to a 45° angle.

Some old framed hand crosscut saws had one post extending downward past the blade for six or eight inches to serve as a handle. This design is used exactly as with the other type except that the right hand is placed below the blade instead of above.

As with almost any tool it is important to use the whole body when using a frame saw. Back, shoulders, arms, even legs should each contribute to the motion, sharing burden so that no one part of the body tires too quickly. Stance is also important. The feet should be placed far enough apart to provide a stable foundation for the moving body, and the position of the feet in relation to the work should be determined by each workman on the basis of both stability and comfort. Proper height of the work in relation to the height of the workman should not be overlooked as a factor in providing stamina.

Time after time the matter of rhythm will be mentioned in connection with using old hand tools and for good reason, particularly in sawing. Hand tools are but extensions of the man, as pointed out by John Ruskin, and must have transmitted to them the natural rhythms of the human body. Rhythm makes the work easier and more pleasant. And with sawing the natural rhythm which fits the workman's personality furnishes a rhythmic, almost musical accompaniment, to his work. It is most satisfying to hear the tone as the crosscut saw slices through the grain when pushed and changes in timbre on the unproductive return stroke; to notice the deeper tone evolve as the blade courses through a board; to hear the higher tone on the last two or three strokes required to sever the stuff.

One advantage of the framed crosscut saw over the later panel saw is that the frame, being of some length, serves as a guide for keeping the blade perpendicular to the wood, a sign of professional work. A perpendicular cut, however, was not always important in the old days. Often a coarse saw would be used to cut quickly a board almost to proper length, then the end would be planed to perfect perpendicularity.

There is some difference in using the panel saw with closed handle which appeared first in Holland in the seventeenth century and soon was adopted by English woodworkers and then taken to the American colonies. Most modern woodworking texts describe the use of this saw, still easily available at any hardware store of the 1970s but it used so sparingly and frequently inexpertly in the mechanized shops of the power-saw era that it seems feasible to repeat basic instructions on its use.

The panel saw is grasped firmly but comfortably in the hand, the upper spur of the handle fitting snugly into the thumb joint. It should be remembered that the design of the handle made the panel saw attractive to seventeenth century wood-

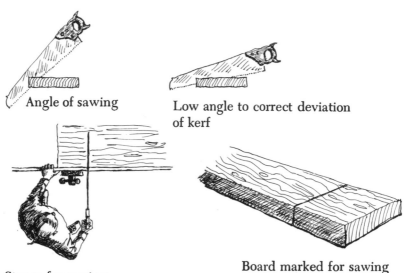

Angle of sawing

Low angle to correct deviation
of kerf

Stance for sawing

Board marked for sawing

workers rather than the wide blade for it is the handle which
gives so much better control over the angle of stroke than is
found in the framed saw. The other hand usually grasps the
board being sawn, even if the board is firmly secured in vise or
by holdfast, for this braces the body, supplementing the support
of the feet and making it possible to put one's whole upper body
behind the motion of the blade.

Another function other than support attaches to the hand
holding the board. Its position is adjacent to the mark for sawing
so that the thumb may be slightly elevated to serve as a guide
for starting the kerf.

To start, the saw blade is placed on the sawing mark at a
45° angle with the end of the raised left thumb pressing
gently against it. Then, as with the framed saw, the blade is
pulled gently over the corner of the board with short strokes
until the kerf is started. When a channel has been formed the
saw is pushed, being held at a 45° angle, until the board is
sawn through. The thumb is only held against the blade until
actual sawing commences.

As with the framed saw, no downward pressure is applied
while sawing; the weight of the saw gives quite enough pres-

sure to sink the teeth in the wood enough to cut. And cutting is the object, not tearing.

There are problems in keeping the one hand panel saw perpendicular; these problems are solved by experience, eventually, but by more mechanical means before experience and instinct are developed. One method is to carefully mark a board on two sides, the top and the edge toward the sawyer, with a marking square. Even this method, however, is not failsafe because the novice sawyer will sometimes twist the supple blade while trying to correct perpendicularity and the finished cut will not be straight. Such miscarriage of accuracy confirms that tools should not be forced but used gently according to design, allowed to follow each its own way, with the craftsman merely contributing energy and direction.

Another method of holding the saw in a perpendicular position is to hold or prop a marking square on the board being sawn so that the saw blade can relate to the perfect square.

Of course, there is absolutely no difference between the panel saw and the framed saw in the need for rhythm, the 45° position of edge to the board or the use of a lower angle to correct a straying kerf.

Ripping with a framed saw requires a somewhat different technique from that used with the crosscut because of differences in frame design. The framed rip saw can only be used with two hands and usually requires that the stuff being sawn be held securely on sawing bench or workbench with holdfast or vise. Crossbars on the rip saw frame serve as handles which are grasped by both hands, one on each side of the centrally placed blade. As with the crosscut saw the rip saw is started with short slicing strokes to create a guiding channel for the blade. After the channel is dug the whole body is put behind the rhythmic motion of the blade and the full blade is moved back and forth to rip the stuff down its length.

An advantage of the framed rip saw is that the horizontal handle is most useful in keeping the kerf straight.

A rather specialized form of the framed rip saw which disappeared with the advent of the automobile is the felloe saw, used by wheelwrights to rough saw the felloes, or fellies, of a wagon wheel. Actually the felloe saw, though a rip saw, is some-

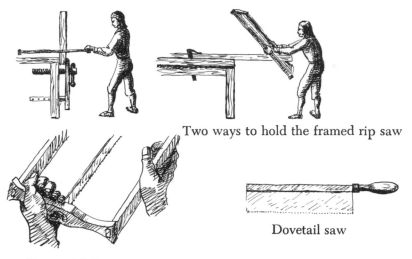

Two ways to hold the framed rip saw

Dovetail saw

Grasp of felloe saw

what akin to the turning saw since it is designed to saw the rather flat arc required in a felloe. As a consequence its blade is narrower than that of the normal rip saw and it is frequently handled in a different manner. Often the thick board from which a felloe is being sawn is fastened to the top of the workbench with a holdfast, its end projecting over the front of the bench. When the felloe saw is used to cut a board in this position the sawyer grasps the side stretcher of the saw with his right hand and the frame end, normally the handle, with the left hand. Motion of the saw in this position is up and down, vertical rather than horizontal. The path of the kerf, matching the marking of the felloe outline, is observed and directed from the top.

Panel rip saws are used exactly like panel crosscut saws.

Both rip and crosscut sawing by hand will be a pleasant and relatively easy task if the craftsman develops the same attitude toward his tools as the eighteenth- and early nineteenth-century craftsmen: that the tool should do the work well and easily because of its design, not because of a strong right arm.

Any hand craftsman should have several each of rip and crosscut saws, the difference being in coarseness of teeth. A 5 or

5½ point saw will cut twice as quickly with the same effort as a 10 point saw. For crosscutting heavier boards and for ripping long boards from a half inch thickness upward at least a 5½ point saw should be used. Where a fairly tight joint is needed, or for ripping shallow notches to fit around cabinet posts or table legs, an 8 or 15 point saw should be used. And since a worker can be no better than his tools, the well-equipped hand woodworker should have at least two crosscut saws and two rip saws, one of each variety of 5½ points and the other of 8 points. Depending on the general type of work he does and the sort of wood he works with he may want one or two others of varying coarseness of teeth.

Of the three backsaws the dovetail and the tenon saw are used exactly as the panel saw. Since both are used to shape tight joints, however, each is 10 point for working fine smooth cuts. The miter saw, while of the same basic design as the other back saws, is always used in a miter box or block and requires a slightly different technique. Since the miter box itself provides a ready made channel the miter saw is always moved horizontal to the floor, never at the 45° angle used with other saws.

When a butt or angled point is being sawn then of course the saw severs the board and cuts slightly into the wooden base of the miter box or block. If, however, a rabbet is being cut to serve as a mortise for shelves or louvres, the board must be scribed with marking gauge or scriber on both edges and the saw kept perfectly level and matched carefully so that the bottom of the kerf will be exactly parallel to the top and bottom of the boards.

When a number of boards must be sawn exactly the same length in the miter box the job is made easier by temporarily fastening a wooden stop on the wooden base of the miter box. This consists only of a small block of wood tacked to the base at

Tenon saw

Marking board for rabbet cut in miter box

Stop for cutting length in miter box

Rabbet saw with fence

the precise distance from the saw blade to match the desired length of the boards. Measuring must be done from the edge of the set of saw teeth, not the blade itself. Once installed, boards being sawn are butted tightly against the stop and the saw used without the need for marking.

There is no problem with controlling depth with the rabbet saw. With this tool the planelike stock of the saw acts efficiently as a depth gauge, and some forms of the rabbet saw are equipped with a fence which, in contact with the edge of a board, serves as a guide. Most rabbet saws have blades with two or three vertical slots in the portion of the steel which penetrates a kerf in the stock. Screws pass through stock and slots so that the points of the blade may be set a designated distance from the bottom of the stock and the screws tightened to hold it in position. Like the miter saw, the rabbet saw is always moved exactly parallel to the floor.

When the rabbet saw is used to cut a mortise for a shelf some distance from the end of a board it is necessary to provide a fence, fastened to the board with clamps, small nails or hold-fast, to guide the saw and assure that the cut will be a perfect right angle to the edge of the board.

In England and the Continent the turning saw still survives in its seventeenth century form with twisted cord and wooden frame and pivoting handles. Since the saw is used with two hands and is easier to use with the blade in a horizontal position, a vise is necessary to hold the work being done. In cutting all manner of hollow shapes the turning saw is used to cut both cross the grain and with the grain, but most of its cutting is with the grain in most shops and it is filed like a rip saw. And because of its unusually narrow blade it is pulled rather than pushed; the angle of teeth should always point toward the sawyer.

Turning cuts are started with the blade perpendicular to the plane of the board, which is not difficult since the blade has between nine and twelve points to the inch and acts as a coarse file when pushed against the stuff several times to start its kerf.

To start, and to continue cutting, the saw handle is held with both hands and pulled toward the sawyer. Many sections of a shaped kerf may be horizontal, or nearly so, which require that a slight sideways pressure be used when cutting sideways, or upward, but the weight of the saw provides enough pressure to cut when the kerf goes downward.

To turn the narrow blade as it cuts a curved line the sawyer merely has to turn his wrist slightly to guide the course of the blade, a technique which is quickly learned with experience.

Acute angles and sharp corners cannot be done with one cut. First an arc is cut as closely as the blade allows to create a rounded corner; then the saw is reversed in the kerf and cut straight to the corner from both directions. Often this requires

Guide on board for rabbet saw

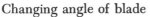

Grasp for turning saw

Changing angle of blade

that the piece being cut out must be severed completely from the rest of the board and after the initial cutting the saw is returned to the corners and sharp angles to true them to the original conception. Many workers prefer to bore holes at places where corners will be, to facilitate using the saw in these tight places.

Because the frame of a turning saw frequently interferes with turning the blade sufficiently to cut certain shapes, the plane of the blade must be turned from time to time in its relation to the frame so that the frame does not rub against the stuff. This is done normally by removing the blade from the kerf, laying the frame on one side or the other, flat on the bench, grasping a handle in each hand and twisting the handles evenly to change the relationship of the plane of the blade and the plane of the frame.

When only a slight change in the angle of the blade is needed to complete a cut it can sometimes be done without removing the blade from the work. First one handle is twisted slightly with one hand while the other hand holds the frame steady, then the other handle is twisted to match and bring the blade to an even plane along its length. Sometimes several of these small adjustments are needed to turn the blade to its final angle.

One must be careful always to sight along the blade after adjusting to make certain that there is no twist from handle to handle. A twisted blade cannot be controlled within the kerf and even a slight twist can quite ruin intended accuracy.

Wooden frames, regardless of how well protected with varnish or linseed oil, are affected by the weather. Such swelling and shrinking has no effect on framed crosscut saw or rip saw, but it can create a frustrating situation in using the turning saw. For when the wood swells and binds the iron or brass posts to which the blade is fastened, the angle of the blade cannot be adjusted when needed. This situation is usually easily remedied by removing the blade and tapping the ends of the posts with a light mallet or block of wood until they may be removed. Once removed the posts may be rubbed with a candle end, a piece of dry soap or with a graphite pencil to provide lubrication, then they are reinserted in the frame. If, after lubrication, the posts still bind they should be removed again and the hole in the frame enlarged carefully with a rat tail file. When using the file only a few strokes should be taken at a time and the post fitted and tried. The post must have some friction to prevent the blade's twisting while in use.

Not all turning cuts originate and finish on the edge of the stuff being worked; frequently interior shapes must be cut and again the frame interferes with inserting the blade through the stuff at the point for cutting. To accomplish this with the framed turning saw the frame must be loosened and the blade detached from one post. Then it is inserted through a previously bored hole, the edge of which coincides at some point with the pattern mark for the interior cut, and again fastened in the end of the post. Then the cord is twisted to tighten the frame and sawing is commenced.

Keyhole saws, with either a straight or a pistol-grip handle, may also be used to cut interior shapes if the cutting is not too extensive. As with the turning saw the handle should be held with both hands while the work is secured in a vise. Keyhole saws, however, are push saws. They are not too suitable for extensive cutting because the blade, though thicker in proportion to width than other unframed saws, does tend to buckle if long strokes are taken, and short strokes require a great deal of time to complete a cut. They are most suitable, as the name suggests, for sawing keyholes.

The most important sawing auxiliary besides the saw rest, already described in conjunction with the workbench, is the miter box or miter block, used to determine accurate angles for picture frames, cabinet molding and other items with angled joints.

Patented miter boxes of great accuracy have been made available by industry since before the year 1900, but the ancient form, easily made in the shop, is quite satisfactory, particularly when mitered corners are planed to absolute accuracy after sawing. The old-fashioned simple miter box consists of three boards, preferably of hardwood, which are nailed together to form a channel which fits the sort of work to be done, generally

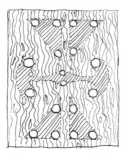

Preparing work for interior cutting (Holes are bored before shaded area is cut out with turning saw)

Sawing angles on miter box

from three to eight inches wide. Many miter boxes over the centuries have been made from ¾"–1" boards, but the use of 1½" boards is generally more satisfactory. The box should be at least a foot long.

After the box itself has been assembled, by nailing or screwing the two vertical boards to the edges of the base, comes the delicate job of sawing the angled kerfs which impart accuracy to the finished miter. Accuracy in marking these cuts is essential and it is well to attend to the ancient admonition that a wise woodworker measures twice and saws once.

First, to determine a 45° angle, the marking square is employed to mark a right angle line across the top edges of the vertical boards about three inches from one end. A careful measurement of the outside width of the box must then be made and this distance measured from the original line down the outside edge of the board where another line is drawn across both boards with the square. If measured carefully the outside edges of the boards and the lines across the boards will form a perfect square. Accurate 45° angles are marked by joining opposite corners with the edge of a rule or straight board and marking these with pencil or scriber. The ends of these angled lines should then be continued, using the square, on the sides of the vertical boards, this mark to guide the kerf downward as the angled cut is made.

A couple of important points must be understood before sawing the 45° angles from the top of the side boards to the top of the base. For one, the edge of the saw must exactly bisect the right angle formed by the original squared marks and the edges of the boards at opposite corners, otherwise the 45° angle will not be exact. Also, the saw must cut exactly perpendicularly down the sides of the box. This last can be controlled by using a back-saw, if one is available, and by tacking a straight 1½″ thick board across the top of the box, one of its edges exactly corresponding to the 45° angled mark. This board will serve to guide the saw in a perpendicular position at the beginning of the cut.

A right angle kerf is easily made by marking a line with the square about three inches from the end of the box opposite the angled kerfs and employing a guide board as before to control the perpendicular direction from top to bottom.

Miter boxes should be fastened or steadied on the bench top while in use. If placed in a permanent position they can be fastened with screws or nails to the bench top, making sure that screw or nail heads are below the upper surface of the base board to prevent scarring any work held inside the box. If not permanently fixed the box may be held in the front vise or may be steadied by pressing it against bench stops while sawing.

Molding or boards to be mitered are placed inside the box and pressed tightly against the wall away from the workman. Then the saw, preferably a backsaw, is placed in the angled kerf and the stuff is sawed through without undue downward pressure.

Some old woodworkers preferred a miter block to a box. This type of jig consists of a two-inch-thick board cut to a right triangle and mounted on an inch-thick board exactly as wide as the distance between the apex of the triangle and its base, the base of the triangle being mounted flush with the edge of the board. This assembly in turn is mounted on another inch-thick board some three or four inches wider than the original with the base of the triangle again coinciding with the edges of both boards. When assembled the miter block consists of two steps with a triangle on top.

To use the miter block the stuff to be cut is laid on the bottom step, its edge pressed tightly against the edge of the top step. A backsaw is then placed against the appropriate edge of the triangle which guides it vertically as well as horizontally.

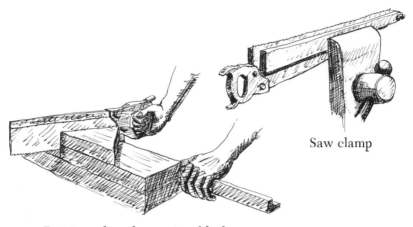

Saw clamp

Position of work on miter block

The first cut on a new miter block must be continued through the top step to the level of the top surface of the bottom step. Thereafter this kerf serves as an added guide to the saw blade.

One of the major secrets of gaining creative pleasure from the use of woodworking tools is keeping them sharp. Saws are not excepted from this requirement even though, if kept properly, they do not need sharpening nearly as often as plane irons or chisels. Saw blades should be oiled lightly by rubbing with a rag into which a little lubricating oil has been soaked as a means of preventing rust, which dulls. When using, extreme care should be taken not to cut through nails or screws.

Sharpening saws is a rather delicate and difficult job, especially with dovetail and tenon saws which may have up to 15 points to the inch. Three steps must be followed and several special tools, one of them easily made in the shop, are needed.

All operations in sharpening a saw are made easier by securing the saw blade in a saw clamp which is held in the vise. Saw clamps are made by fastening two thin boards, about three inches wide and six inches longer than the saw blade, together at one end with a bolt or screw. The saw blade is inserted between these two boards with an inch or so of the blade's width extending beyond the top edge of the clamp. Large two-man crosscut saws do not require either clamp or vise; they can be held over the top of a stump and sharpened in the woods.

First of all, the saw blade must be top-jointed, joint referring to the evenness of the points along a straight line from handle to end of blade. This is done with a flat mill or mill bastard file held in an easily made block which consists of two narrow boards, about a foot long, nailed together along their edges to form a right angle. The file is placed flat on the inside surface of one board then the block is reversed so that the file rests flatly on the saw points and the other board in the block serves as a fence to keep the file horizontal. Jointing is done by merely running the file along the length of the blade, with downward pressure deriving only from the weight of file and block, until all teeth are of the same length.

Sharpening is done with a small six inch triangular file for hand saws or with a larger saw file or twelve inch mill bastard file for two-man crosscut saws. Saw files have a mill bastard cut, or diagonal teeth which are not crossed, and a wedge-shape section with a rounded base. In past days, when all files were made by hand, it was possible to buy triangular files in which the cut was coarse at the point and progressed to a finer cut at the tang, a type considered ideal for sharpening saws. It is not essential to have this type file, however.

In filing hand crosscut saws the file is held horizontally and at about a 45° angle to the plane of the blade for most saws. Filing is done gently and horizontally with only slight pressure against the front edge of one tooth, while at the same time filing the back edge of the adjacent tooth. Alternate teeth are filed in this way from back to front. Then the saw is reversed in the vise and those teeth not filed are sharpened. Care must be taken not to file beyond the point of each tooth; otherwise the jointing will be ruined, preventing the shorter teeth from cutting.

For rip saws the file is held at a 90° angle to the plane of the blade in order to sharpen teeth to the required chisel edge for ripping along the grain. Again, the file is used gently to preserve the joint. Frequently in olden times the teeth on the first four inches of a rip saw would be filed for crosscutting, to take care of knots encountered in ripping.

There are other factors which affect the efficiency of both crosscut and rip saws, factors which are almost forgotten in the Industrial Age but which were most important in maintaining peak efficiency in the days of hand tools. One of the factors is the rake with the front angle of its teeth 90° to the line of the width of it at its base.

Rake is determined by the angle of the front of the tooth to a line running along its base. The more this angle leans toward the front on push saws or the back on pull saws the more rake that tooth has. For either crosscutting or ripping soft woods, such as pine or fir, a saw should have considerable rake with the front angle of its teeth 90° to the line of the base. A rip saw, indeed, may be filed 10° forward of the 90° angle when used for soft woods. For sawing hardwood, however, the teeth may be filed between 45° and 90°, the lower angle to be used for exceptionally hard woods where it functions with a slicing action in the crosscut saw or a filing action with the rip saw. Crosscut saws for hardwood may have 10° less rake than rip saws for the same wood.

Relative length of tooth is also determined by the type of wood to be sawn. Longer teeth do a more satisfactory job of sawing soft or gummy wood since the spaces between teeth will carry away more sawdust with each stroke. The differences of rake and length of teeth were not so important to the carpenter of olden days who worked with only a few woods during his lifetime. The cabinetmaker or joiner, however, paid much attention to such details as a source of both efficiency and accuracy in his saw cuts.

The normal triangular file, with equilateral faces at 60° to one another, is not suitable for all degrees of rake, and the lack of a source for ordering special files in modern times creates a problem for the modern woodworker who enjoys following pre-industrial methods. Perhaps the best solution to this dilemma is for the modern man to purchase suitable types of patternmakers' files, most of them available in finer cut than is necessary for saw filing, but with the advantage of having many shapes suitable for filing different rakes in hand saws.

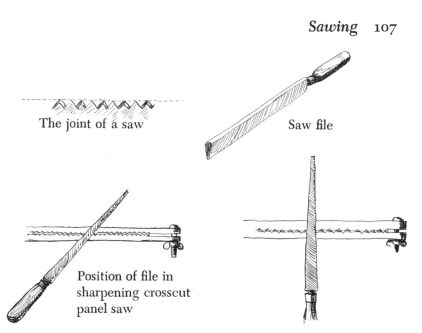

The joint of a saw

Saw file

Position of file in sharpening crosscut panel saw

Position of file in sharpening rip saw

Rake of tooth for soft and hard wood

Relative lengths of saw teeth to width of base

After jointing and filing, the teeth of a saw must be set as already described. Since about 1890 a number of foolproof mechanical sets have appeared on the market and most have now disappeared because of the demise of the hand saw as a primary tool in commercial and home workshops. Before the 1890s the saw sharpener used a set of ancient form shaped roughly like a small paddle with an inch-wide blade some $\frac{3}{16}''$ thick at the base and about $\frac{1}{16}''$ thick at its end. Most of the old sets had two or three slots cut into each edge, the slots corresponding in width to the thickness of the saw blade to be set. The tapering thickness of the set itself was, of course, to accommodate the points on saws of differing coarseness. A thickness

Setting with 18th-century saw set

of $\frac{1}{16}''$ would be used on a sixteen point saw; $\frac{3}{16}''$ thickness is about the width of the base of each tooth on a 5½ point saw.

Old type saw sets are no longer made and difficult to find in antique shops. Any handworker, however, can make his own by cutting a half-inch slot with a hack saw in the edge of a metal bar of proper thickness. There is no heresy involved here for the purist. Old timers often used an expedient means of solving problems.

Saws, rip or crosscut, for general work usually have alternate teeth set at about a 15° angle from the plane of the saw blade, with perhaps 5° more for cutting soft woods and 5° less for cutting hard woods. Very gummy woods require about a 20° set to keep the saw from binding and to allow the gummy sawdust to escape with each stroke.

Actual setting is accomplished by placing the proper slot of the saw set over a tooth and levering the handle of the saw set downward to bend the tooth to its desired set. A minimum of experience will soon allow the craftsman to develop a feel of the pressure used in setting so that he soon will be able to administer equal pressure when setting each individual tooth.

After alternate teeth have been set on one side the saw is reversed in the vise and the remaining teeth are set. After setting, the overall set should be checked by sighting along the edge of the blade. If any teeth are set too far they may be reset by tapping on the outside surface with a light hammer. Those not set far enough may be corrected with the saw set.

Two-man crosscut saws are set with a hammer of about

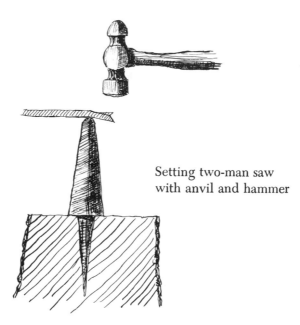

Setting two-man saw
with anvil and hammer

two pounds weight while the base of the tooth rests on a small stake anvil of special design which may be driven into a stump or log in the woods. A 10° set is sufficient for the large saws. It should be remembered that dowel saws have no set.

In the generation since World War II, which marked the real demise of hand saws among carpenters and lumbermen, the general attitude toward hand sawing is that it is an onerous operation from which mankind has been saved because of the development and availability of power saws of various types and sizes. It is quite true that electrical and internal combustion engines remove the need for some effort in sawing. But while they do the job much more quickly, they also remove the pleasure and the feeling of oneness between the man and his tool. The man who understands hand saws, and uses saws specifically suited to his work and maintains them as a good saw should be maintained, will enjoy far greater pleasure, withal less production, with hand saws than with power saws. The rhythms developed, the gentle sounds, the feeling of individual accomplishment in using hand saws can become intellectual and esthetic discoveries instead of work.

CHAPTER V

Hewing

ADZ AND BROADAX in all forms may easily be given the distinction of being the first finishing tools. These two were probably used concurrently over the ages to produce man's first lumber as opposed to timber; to provide him ultimately with the delight of working with pieces of wood which could be neatly joined together as an artistic creation rather than an expedient; and quite possibly to stimulate his inherent genius to improve his still primitive woodworking technology by inspiring the invention of chisel and drawknife, saw and plane. But in addition to technology, the hewing tools possibly inspired him also to develop artistic, professional technique. Masters of the adz in all its forms, and artists with the broadax and hatchet, however, often preferred their relatively primitive tools because precise technique allowed them to eschew the more technologically developed plane and drawknife and produce a finely smoothed board with only the tool and their hands, *sans* bench, *sans* vise, *sans* holdfast and clamp. They hewed to the line and let the chips fall where they might.

Hewing is not a complicated process. All that is needed is a sharp tool, a clear mark on the stuff being worked and a good eye which is developed only through experience.

The broadax and its little brother, the hatchet, come in many related forms, some reflecting cultural provenience and others special uses. Most have blades at least two or three times as wide as the poll and eye, a characteristic which gives the tool its descriptive name. On some, however, the blade flares equally up

Broadax and hatchet—goosewing and medieval

and down, on others, such as the mainly German goosewing broadax, the edge flares only along the handle and on some ancient and medieval forms the blade flares upward to a point, vaguely reminding one of a bird in flight. Each is used in the same general manner with no difficulty once we get used to it.

Broadaxes are used on large timbers and hatchets on small boards. Part of the technique of using these tools is to properly mark the line in the stuff to be hewn, a procedure which is somewhat involved in dealing with large tree trunks but quite simple in the case of boards.

A tree trunk which must be hewn square for a cabin log, bridge timber, house stringer or sill or, in latter days, for railroad ties, must first be stripped of its bark. This job is done usually with barking iron, peeling chisel or spud. Spuds and peeling chisels are of similar design, the peeling chisel being no more than a large chisel with a long socketed handle which makes the overall tool about three feet long. It is pushed under the bark of the tree to peel it off. The spud looks something like a three foot long spoon with a flat bowl which is sharpened on its edges. Barking irons resemble the spuds except that the handles are perpendicular to the shank. All function exactly alike.

The peeled log is then rolled onto two smaller logs, one at each end, to raise it so that a horizontal line through its center

Position of log with dogs

Barking with barking iron

Chalk line and reel

Marking with chalk line

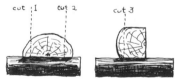

Positions for hewing split logs

is about at the height of the axman's knee. At this height the log may be hewn comfortably without too much bending of the back. It is well worth the time required to raise a large log to a comfortable height because it can be hewn more quickly and accurately and stamina is increased.

Once raised into position the large log is fastened to the smaller transverse logs with a dog at each end. The dog is essentially a large square staple of iron, in one form with one hinged point, which has one point driven into the log and the other in the transverse log to secure the large log while it is being worked.

Now the log is marked down its length, employing a light string coated with chalk or charcoal dust. This string is usually kept on a small reel which can be held in one hand as the string is pulled out to the length of the log and with a handle to turn, as on a fishing reel, when the string must be rewound. Chalk or charcoal dust is applied to the string by dipping the string into a small box filled with the dust or drawing it through holes or slots in the dust filled box. Sometimes an ingenious hewer might combine box and reel so that the dust is applied automatically as the string is unreeled.

To mark the line to be hewn the string is stretched tautly along the length of the log and snapped to transfer chalk or charcoal dust to the white moist surface of the debarked trunk. When two men are at hand and the log not too long, the string can be held by a man at each end of the log while one picks it up and snaps it to mark the hewing line. But usually the log is nicked by an ax at each end and splinters are driven into the nicks. The string is tied tautly between the two splinters, snapped and rewound on the reel.

Often large logs were split down the middle before being hewn for log cabins, both to diminish the number of trees to be felled and to provide one fairly smooth surface which needed a minimum of hewing. Half logs, after having the bark removed, are always laid on the supporting logs with split side down when being marked with the string and hewn. Hewing then provides a flat side on which the half log can be set while hewing the broad middle portion and the split surface.

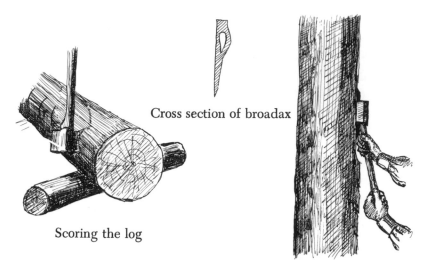

Cross section of broadax

Scoring the log

Curve of handle showing grasp

Actual hewing consists of two separate operations. First the log is scored, on the side to be hewn, with a felling ax, the cut being about an inch deep. After being scored the broadax is brought into play to hew a flat surface even with the depth of the scoring. If more wood must be removed the hewn surface is once more scored with the felling ax and once again hewn with the broadax. Ax marks observed on old hewn timbers are always the result of scoring with the felling ax, for the broadax, properly used, can make a surface so smooth that it might almost have been planed.

Scoring is done most easily by standing on top of the log and using the felling ax as though the log were to be bucked. The ax is swung just as in bucking, the only difference being that no chips are removed and the axman moves sideways down the log after each stroke. As with bucking, the scores are made at an angle to allow the ax to penetrate the wood more easily. Usually both sides of the log are scored before hewing commences.

Before one can understand the special technique of hewing one must understand the design and function of the broadax. It is a heavy instrument, its fourteen-pound weight adding to its efficiency. The edge is preferably straight and, although some well used broadaxes develop a slightly curved blade from many sharpenings, the straight edge should be preserved for greater efficiency. Unlike the felling ax the broadax is sharpened on one side only, like a chisel, the resulting basil, or bezel, being usually on the right side. The handle is short, about two feet in length, and it is curved to the right, the curve starting immediately at the eye. Its left side surface is a flat plane with the eye swelling only on the right. In effect the broadax head is a nine-inch chisel blade affixed to a curved handle set at a right angle to the head on a line curved from the edge.

There is no swinging with the broadax. Using it properly is a matter of lifting and letting fall, the razor-sharp edge and the weight being allowed to perform its function, the axman only guiding the course of the edge.

To hew, the axman stands with his left knee touching the surface to be hewn, his right hand grasping the handle at the eye, the hand touching the head itself, and with the left hand grasping the handle some six inches from its end. In this position the axman lifts the head six or eight inches, keeping the edge parallel to the log, sights where the edge should enter at about the bottom of the scoring cuts and pushes downward to remove the wood between the scoring cuts. Hewing should start at the end of the log to which the axman faces. The axman moves backward as he hews and uses the freshly hewn surface as a guide for continued hewing.

Hewing with the broadax is not difficult if the axman sights each cut carefully and makes certain that the flat plane of the left side of the broadax head is kept precisely parallel to the surface being hewn.

Hatchets require a slightly different technique only because they are one-handed tools used on boards much smaller than logs. Although a hatchet handle is as long as that of a hand ax the hatchet is not swung like an ax, and the handle normally is grasped by the right hand next to the head as with the broadax. When a board is to be hewn it is held with the left hand in an upright position and scoring is applied with the hatchet. Then, starting at the bottom, the wood between the scoring is hewn off, the hatchet rising after each stroke. As with the broadax, the hatchet is pushed, rather than swung, downward. Also, the flat left side of the hatchet head is kept parallel to the line being

Position for using broadax

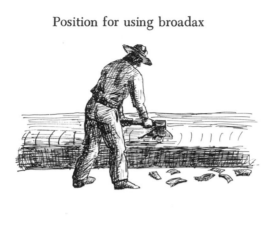

Grasp of hatchet showing
board and scoring

Half hatchet, shingling hatchet, lathing hatchet, Kent ax

hewn. The basiled edge should be kept razor sharp if accurate hewing is to be done.

There are other tools called hatchets but which are not designed to do the hewing required of broadax and true hatchet. Half-hatchets, shingling hatchets and lathing hatchets all have knife edges, rather than chisel edges, and all have an elongated poll which may be used for a hammer. Indeed, all are combination tools and all, despite the designation of hatchet, are used essentially for chopping rather than hewing.

The hatchet, though a specialized tool in the British Isles and Western Europe, should not be despised as a general building tool. Until World War II, or later in some areas, carpenters in the Slavic countries built houses employing only the hatchet, which was used to replace both hammer and saw.

Adzes, two-handed and one-handed, are used to hew a smoother surface than either broadax or hatchet. The two-handed sort is known as the foot adz, doubtless because the adzman's foot often serves to guide the course of the razor-sharp edge. Smaller adzes are known as hand adzes or carpenter's adzes, with a few specialized types designated cooper's adzes.

In effect, adzes of any size are large heavy chisels with a handle which lies perpendicular to the plane of the blade. As with the broadax the edge is straight and basiled, the basil being on the side from which the handle protrudes. The adz eye is a tapered socket about three inches deep which is offset from the thin curved blade with the wide part of the taper on the outside of the curve, the socket extending on the inside. Adz eyes are deep in order to keep the handle steady in use, otherwise the tool could not be used precisely. The handle itself may be either straight or with a slight curve toward the edge or with a double curve, first away from the edge and then back toward it. There is a swelling on the end of the handle which is held in the eye, the taper of the swelling exactly fitting the inside taper of the eye. This makes it possible to easily remove the handle for sharpening the edge on its basiled side by grindstone, an operation which is impossible when the handle is in place.

Timbers to be adzed may be laid flat on a level piece of ground; no trestles are needed as for broadaxing. The hewing is

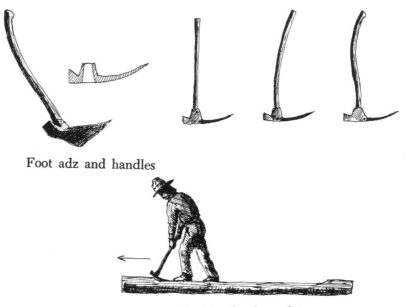

Foot adz and handles

Position for foot adzing

done with the adzman standing on top of the timber and swinging the tool toward himself. Scoring is not necessary, but sometimes a round log might be scored with a felling ax before employing the adz.

Stance is important in using a foot adz. The left foot is placed about eighteen inches in front of the right, with the right foot pointing at about a 45° angle to the left. Both hands grasp the handle, the left hand on its end, the right directly below it.

A short swing is used, the adz head moving in a precise arc only about a foot in each swing. Adzing starts about two feet from the end of the timber behind the adzman, the tool being swung under the sole of the left shoe, the chip being no more than a quarter inch thick. After each swing the adzman moves forward about three inches and swings again to hew another surface on the same plane created by the previous cut. Once the proper rhythm of swinging and moving forward is established and the position of the back is maintained, hewing with the foot adz becomes a pleasure. When the timber has been hewn to its end the adzman reverses his position and levels off the two feet not yet hewn on the end where hewing was started.

As with most tools, the sharp edge and the five- to six-pound weight of the adz head do most of the work with the adzman merely lifting and guiding. Because of the constant proximity of the edge of the left foot adzing can be a dangerous exercise, but once confidence is developed one tends to forget the danger. It was a common sport in the American backwoods for an expert adzman to bet that he could split his shoe sole neatly in two without touching either the timber or the foot inside the shoe. Among the experienced experts more bets were won than toes split, but experience is quite necessary to undertake such a challenge.

In order to become proficient, an adzman should be certain that the handle of his tool fits his height. A miscalculation of only a quarter of an inch can cripple a man for life, and the length of the handle is an important factor in controlling the depth of successive cuts, each placed exactly where it should be placed.

Hand adzes differ slightly from the larger foot adz both in form and in technique needed. Most American, British and Western European hand adzes have a proportionately longer blade than the foot adz and a longer poll for better balance. The curve of the blade varies for different uses, with the blades of some forming almost a half circle. All hand adzes of American or British derivation have a short handle, no more than six to eight inches long, but modern Portuguese and Greek types have a handle of at least a foot long. One Greek type differs also in having a very short broad poll and an angled rather than curved blade. Eighteenth century British and American adzes had a long eye similar to the foot adz but without the taper; more modern mass-produced carpenter's and cooper's adzes were made with a virtual socket which extended over the handle at least three inches.

In use the carpenter's adz is grasped with the right hand directly adjacent to the head while the stuff being hewn is held upright on the bench or a block of wood by the left hand. Instead of being swung the small adz is more or less pushed downward in a series of rotary strokes, the action of the arm being

Hand adz showing grasp

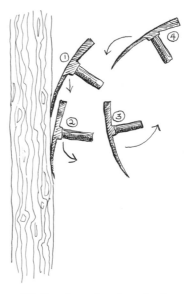

Motion in using hand adz

much like the action of a driving rod operating a wheel. Most of the work is the result of a sharp edge and weight as with all chopping and hewing tools.

Hewing begins at the bottom of the stuff being worked and progresses upward. When a piece is hewn to within a couple of inches of the top the piece is turned upside down for finishing.

Hand adzes can be used to rough out shapes such as chair arms and window arches, sometimes so precisely that planing is unnecessary.

There is a type of adz called a gouge adz because of its curved edge. This type is found in both foot and hand adzes. The foot gouge adz may be used to hollow out logs for watering troughs or dugout canoes, using the same technique employed with the regular foot adz. Hand gouge adzes are well suited for hollowing out dough or salad bowls and for shaping the inside of barrel staves.

Broadaxes and all types of adzes have virtually disappeared from the tool kits of modern woodworkers in America and most of Western Europe but are used increasingly by wood sculptors.

Only the hatchet, of all the hewing tools, is used by late twentieth century carpenters of the Western world and only for rare trimming jobs on joists or studs. Most carpenters would not even recognize a hand adz, but many might find it most convenient from time to time in hewing house timbers in spots to effect a better joint. The hand adz is much easier to use than power saw, sander or chisel in many instances, but it is doubtful that its use will be revived.

The same admonition must be given to hewers as to users of the other cutting tools: keep the edges of hewing tools razor sharp for efficiency and safety. All should be ground from time to time on a slowly turning grindstone, but this is necessary only at infrequent intervals. Edges are usually maintained with an oil stone and a fine honing stone. Files are not used because the temper of hewing tools is generally harder than that of chopping axes and a file will not cut the metal.

The Bible disparages the hewers of wood, putting them in the same category as drawers of water, a rather lowly occupation. Hewing, however, requires great artistry; as much as playing the right note on a musical instrument or recreating the relative position of lines and planes in painting a portrait. As a consequence hewing is rather a satisfying activity and properly done by a handcraftsman in wood can save much of the time and effort required for using saw or chisel.

CHAPTER VI

Boring

A NUMBER of various tools were used in olden days for boring holes in wood. Most have been replaced either entirely or partially by the electric drill, and some disappeared from the shop of the woodworker a generation or two before the electric drill was developed.

Probably the simplest of all boring tools is the awl, used in drilling materials other than wood and designated a brad awl by the eighteenth century carpenter when it was used to drill holes in thin lumber so that brads or broad-headed nails would not split the stuff when they were driven through it. The brad awl is no more than a slim steel rod about 2½″ long inserted in a nearly spherical handle and sharpened to an obtuse edge on one end. It is used by placing the point on a board where the small hole is desired and rotating it with a reciprocal motion until a hole is drilled.

Two drilling devices, which have seldom been used since about 1840, were inherited from the Stone Age. One is the pump drill, the other the bow drill. Both operate by reciprocal action, the pump drill being a simple machine powered by centrifugal force, the bow drill being powered by hand.

A pump drill consists of a wooden spindle 15″–18″ long with a drill point inserted in one end or, in later days, a simple chuck, and a hole drilled through the spindle about an inch from the other end. Some 3″ above the point a flywheel of wood or stone is placed and secured around the spindle, wooden flywheels being from 3″–5″ in diameter and an inch thick, stone

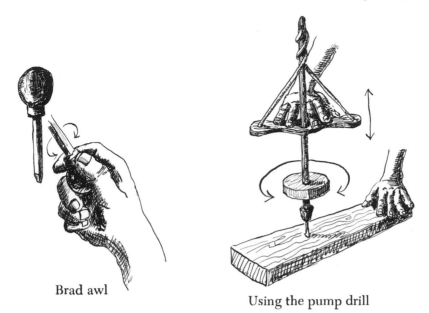

Brad awl

Using the pump drill

wheels being 1½″–2″ thick and about 2″ in diameter. The mechanism is completed by a handle 8″ long, bored to fit loosely around the spindle and held in place just above the flywheel by a thong which is attached to each end of the handle after being inserted through the hole in the spindle's top end.

Pump drills are used to bore very small holes, usually no larger than ⅛″ in diameter. The bits are known as diamond bits because the end is flattened roughly into a diamond shape, the lower sides of the diamond being sharpened to knife edges. To hold the point in place when starting the workman uses a brad awl to make a slight depression in the stuff and places the bit point in this before preparing the drill for action.

Preparation is quite simple. With the point in place and the right hand loosely held on the handle, the spindle is twisted so that the thongs reaching from spindle to handle are twisted around the spindle, at the same time drawing the handle upward. When the handle will go no farther, the spindle is released and the handle pushed gently downward, causing the thong to unwind and the spindle to rotate. When the handle reaches its bottom point the pressure on it is released and centrifugal force from the flywheel winds the thong in the opposite direction and causes the handle to rise once again so that it may be pushed downward again to repeat the action.

Very little practice will teach a worker to develop a rhythm which allows him to operate the pump drill almost without effort, the weight of the right hand providing enough power to unwind and wind the thong. Proper rhythm, however, is the secret to success.

Boring holes with the pump drill is a rather slow process but one which results in a far neater hole than from the brad awl. Pump drills were more widely used by silver-, gold- and coppersmiths than by woodworkers, but the ingenious device was usually found in fine cabinet shops while almost never found in the carpenter's tool kit.

The bow drill, also an ancient device, was commonly used in cabinet shops (though seldom by carpenters) until chucks were improved for the brace and bit, in the early years of the nineteenth century, to allow bits of various sizes to be exchanged quickly and easily. Bow drills consist of a wooden chuck about four inches long equipped with a spindle which fits into a loosely rotating knob on top. The bow, of steel or wood, is about two feet long, sometimes with a handle and sometimes not, strung with a loose leather thong or linen cord which is two to three inches longer than the bow.

In use, the bow string is wrapped once around the spindle and the bit placed in position with the left hand holding the knob on top of the chuck. The bow is then pulled away from the chuck to tighten the cord and pushed and pulled to rotate the chuck on a reciprocal basis, the left hand lightly pressing the chuck and bit downward with each rotation.

Often the bow drill has several chucks, each with a center bit or diamond bit permanently fastened into it. Knobs are usually removable so that one knob may be used for a number of chucks with varying sized bits. Because it operates by reciprocal motion this type of boring device is only suitable for relatively thin stuff.

Both pump and bow drill actually scrape holes rather than cut them as with other types of bits which drill with a continuous rotary motion.

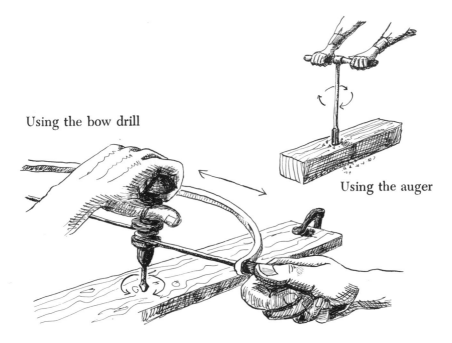

Using the bow drill

Using the auger

At a very early time the auger became the first boring device that was turned continuously in one direction, usually clockwise, to bore a hole. The auger is much more simple in concept than either pump or bow drill but is more effective on thick boards and in boring larger holes. It consists merely of a long bit with one of several different type points and a transverse handle into which the shank of the bit, of square or rectangular section, is inserted and sometimes clinched.

Using an auger, particularly before the year 1800, was — and still is — tiring, vexing work. Yet this tool became the principle boring tool for workers in heavy timber (that is, housewrights, carpenters and shipbuilders) because it employs the weight of the human body and the strength of both arms in boring a hole. Also of utmost importance, its continuous clockwise motion allows the use of a bit which cuts rather than scrapes.

Three cutting type bits were used. First was the shell bit, a semicylindrical bit 3″–4″ long wrought on the end of a 6″ or 8″ shank, with the end and left hand edge of the half cylinder sharpened to a knife edge. When placed on a board, perhaps in a shallow depression made with a chisel to facilitate starting, the shell bit is pressed toward the wood and the handle turned three or four complete revolutions. At this point the bit is removed and all wood shavings are emptied from the hole, perhaps by picking out with a brad awl. The advantage of the shell bit over the diamond bit is, of course, that it cuts instead of scrapes and that the length of the bit guides its course straight through the board once the hole is started. Still, it takes a good while to bore a hole through a one-inch board with auger and shell bit.

The spoon bit is a little easier to use in the auger but requires some preparation. It is similar in shape to the shell bit, but instead of having an open end it has the end closed in a spoon shape. The sharpened rounded end cuts more easily and a sharpened edge, as on the shell bit, maintains the size of the hole as the bit passes through the stuff. But the spoon bit cuts much more easily as a reamer rather than a drill and usually it is best to start the hole with a smaller bit which penetrates for a half inch into the wood. If boring becomes difficult, after the spoon bit has penetrated for an inch or so, then the smaller bit may be used briefly again.

Smaller bits always cut more easily merely because there is less wood to be removed with the effort expended in each twist of the auger handle. Accordingly the ancient, medieval and early modern woodworker often used a pod bit to bore small holes as a guide for larger holes with other type bits. The pod bit is a small rod which has been flattened on its end to form a blade, then pointed, then twisted so that the point forms a primitive screw and the flattened blade is given a lesser twist. It is not suitable for cutting large holes since it lacks the knife-edged blade of shell and spoon bits, but it has other advantages. For one, the screw point serves to draw the bit into the wood and certainly fixes the bit in one place at the beginning of boring; for another, the twisted blade helps remove chips from the hold. It is not suitable for deep holes but may be considered a direct ancestor of the later twist bit.

Possibly the most efficient bit used by early woodworkers is the center bit, another direct ancestor of the modern twist bit.

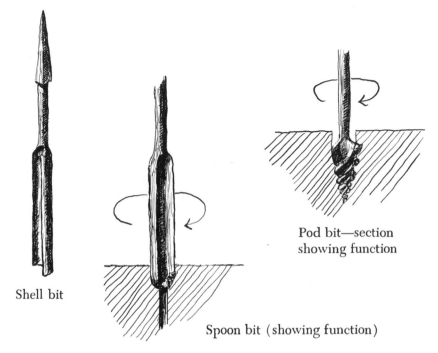

Pod bit—section
showing function

Shell bit

Spoon bit (showing function)

Its name is derived from a spike which protrudes from a flattened blade, the blade having a rotary cutting scribe extending from one edge and a horizontal cutting surface on the opposite side. It is designed only for a continuously rotary motion.

The spike of the center bit holds the tool in position, the cutting spike circumscribes the area to be removed and the cutting surface removes the wood from this area, in a most ingenious and efficient manner. When used in an auger, however, the center bit requires constant downward pressure, far more than furnished by the weight of the tool. Also, since its blade is quite short it is difficult to bore a straight hole for any distance with the center bit. In use its vertical position is kept by relating it to a standard such as the corner of a building, a door or window post or a framing square propped up with blocks against the stuff being bored.

Experienced woodworkers soon learn to use vertical and horizontal surfaces in the shop or near the working area as guides to hold certain tools in a horizontal or vertical position.

Center bit in use

Twist bit (showing function)

It was not until the early years of the nineteenth century that a really efficient boring bit was developed in the form of the twist, or scotch, bit.

Since the twist bit is still commonly used with a brace no detailed description of its form or technique is needed. Suffice it to say that the combination of screw point, cutting edges and twisted blade pulls it into the wood, cuts the hole and removes the shavings by the twisting action of the blade. Automatic removal of the shavings is one of the major improvements of the twist bit.

Twist bits come in all sizes from ¼″ to 2½″. Also they come in lengths up to about three feet for boring peg or bolt holes through heavy building timbers and for other uses.

For holes smaller than a quarter inch when pump or bow drills are not suitable or convenient, the gimlet is employed. This is no more than a small hand auger with a bit which is something of a combination of the pod bit and the twist bit. Its widest use since the year 1800 has been to bore starting holes for wood screws. It is still used extensively in Europe and is available in most hardware stores of the late twentieth century.

Although apparently discontinued during the eighteenth century, there is another form of auger used by housewrights

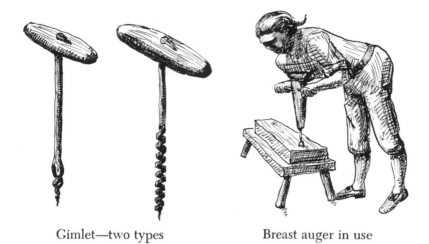

Gimlet—two types   Breast auger in use

and shipwrights, millwrights, wheelwrights and carpenters in medieval times and earlier. The breast auger is much like the regular auger except that it is equipped with a rotating knob on an extension on top of the handle. This knob is placed on the chest, usually with a pad between knob and flesh, so that the weight of the body can be used to hold the bit straight and to apply more downward pressure to make the bit cut. It is more efficient than the regular auger with the crude bits used before the nineteenth century.

Augers are still utilized for certain rare jobs in the latter half of the twentieth century and auger bits (all of twist) and auger handles are still manufactured by a few tool makers. The growing incidence of frame buildings that are nailed rather than pegged and the convenience of wire fencing, steel and concrete bridges and other changes in building technology have almost relegated this ancient tool to oblivion. Its function has been taken over by the brace, supposedly of ancient Oriental origin, which also utilizes interchangeable twist bits, countersinks, screwdriver bits and twist drills of the type used for drilling metal. Braces, greatly improved in design since the early 1800s, are still easily available. They are still commonly used in the 1970s for special boring jobs but this last holdout of the hand wood-boring devices is fast being replaced by the electric drill.

Modern braces, made of steel with rotating wooden handle and head, are distinguished from the earliest braces of the fifteenth century mainly by a most efficient shell chuck which receives and clamps any size bit with a long pyramidal end on the shank. Also, most modern braces include a ratchet on the chuck which allows the sweep to be moved in either direction or in a partial circle, a valuable convenience when the brace is used in removing wood screws or in boring holes in tight corners. Otherwise, the brace used today is used in exactly the same manner as early braces. Its advantage in boring is that it allows a continuous rotation of the bit in a clockwise direction, thereby improving on the intermittent rotation of the auger or the reciprocating motion of pump and bow drills.

Before the invention of the twist, or scotch bit, with its screw point which pulls the cutter into the wood, braces were used most widely to make starting holes in timber which would then be reamed out larger with augers equipped with spoon bits, according to W. L. Goodman in his excellent book, *The History of Woodworking Tools*. At one time the brace and bit were termed a piercer, according to Mr. Goodman, which confirms his theory of the tool's original function.

Since the brace is still a common tool, little is said of the technique of its use. The head, which rotates, is held in the left hand and the sweep is actuated by the right hand. Little pressure is required for boring holes with a twist bit up to three quarters of an inch, but larger bits do require supplementary pressure simply because the screw point cannot always overcome the resistance of a wide cutter. Pressure may be applied by pushing the left arm downward when the bit is vertical, or more satisfactorily by leaning over the head and using the weight of the body to provide additional pressure. In this position the chest is pressed against the right hand which serves to pad the chest and prevent a rather sore breastbone. If the stuff being bored is held in a vise the hole is cut horizontally and either the chest or the shoulder can be placed against the left hand and the strength of body and legs can be used to apply requisite pressure.

The main difference between using the older type brace with wooden stock and chuck and the new, still extant, steel

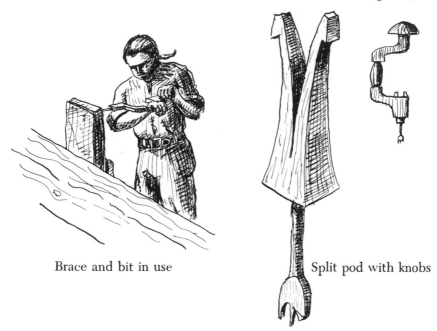

Brace and bit in use   Split pod with knobs

brace with ratcheted shell chuck is in the insertion of interchangeable bits. Braces from the fifteenth until the end of the
eighteenth century had a wooden chuck which was no more
than a tapered square hole in the end of the stock opposite the
head. Bits were individually equipped with wooden pads into
which the bit shank was fixed, and the pad, shaped to fit the
chuck, was merely jambed into the chuck. On occasion the
small end of the pad extended through the chuck and was
secured by a wooden pin inserted crosswise through the
extension.

Later pads were sometimes split down the middle and a
small knob formed on the outside of each leg of the split. When
pressed together the pad may be inserted in the open-ended
chuck and then released so that the knobs spring apart and lock
the pad in place. The spring pad is a relatively rare but quite
ingenious device which can be made by any woodworker. It
was found mostly in the Scandinavian countries in other times.

About the end of the eighteenth century two other type
chucks were developed. One consisted of placing a screw

through the chuck which secured the somewhat loose pad and also made the pad easy to remove. Later versions of this screw chuck used a metal thumbscrew which was inserted through a brass or iron collar which surrounded the wooden chuck. The metal screw could be tightened against the metal shank of the bit, obviating the need for the somewhat awkward pad.

Later still the spring clip chuck was developed in England. This consisted of a brass collar fitted over the wooden chuck with a cavity cast to fit the squared metal shank of the bit. Inside the collar was a hooked spring actuated by a button which extended through the collar. Bit shanks were made with a small notch which was engaged by the spring hook when inserted in the chuck. One merely pressed the button to release the bit. Users of braces equipped with spring hooks must use bits with notched shanks or modify other square shanked bits by filing a proper notch in the shank.

In the middle of the nineteenth century, when metal-stocked braces were being adopted, the English produced a split socket chuck which was closed with a thumbscrew and can be used with any square shanked bit, notched or unnotched. This proved to be a great convenience merely because the manufacturers of spring-hook-chucked braces placed the notches in the bits they furnished with arbitrary whimsy, so that one manufacturer's bits could not fit into a competitor's brace. Notches, however, are easily changed with a small triangular file.

The purpose of boring a hole with augers or braces and bits is not always just to penetrate a piece of stuff for the accommodation of bolt or peg, nor is a hole always bored perpendicularly to a surface. Boring tools were often used to remove a major part of the wood in an intended mortise or to form a round mortise bored at an angle to receive the round tenon of a Windsor chair or bench leg. In special types of woodworking, such as shipbuilding or making oak cannon carriages, very long holes sometimes had to be bored at precise angles. All these operations require special techniques or auxiliary devices, of a simple nature in every instance, but essential for gaining the full potential of boring tools.

Spring chuck diagram

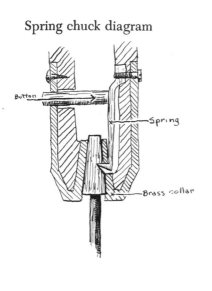

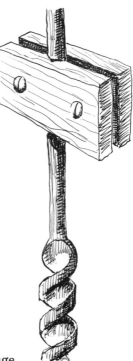

Block type depth gauge

Gauging the depth of a hole, as for preparing a mortise, may be done easily with any one of several devices which in older times were invariably made in the shop as needed. One, the most commonly used, consists of two small wooden blocks an inch wide, two inches long and half an inch thick. Each has a V shaped slot an eighth of an inch deep sawn across the width at its center. These blocks are placed on the shank of the bit and fastened together with a small wood screw at each end. The distance between the bottom of these boards and the cutter of the bit should match the intended depth of the mortise. When the bit cuts its hole it will stop automatically when the blocks reach the top surface of the board. Stop blocks may be easily removed and used on a number of bits of various sizes and types.

A small springy wire may serve the same purpose in any type brace and bit from the earliest to the present. The end of the wire is inserted between pad and chuck or between shank and chuck and the pad jambed in and secured or the chuck tightened, leaving the wire to extend beyond the end of the bit. Then one measures from the base of the screw point on the end of the bit up the wire to a distance equal to the intended depth of the hole and cuts the wire at this point. The wire is then bent gently outward until its point is about a half inch from the bit. With this simple device in place the hole is bored until the end of the wire scrapes the surface of the stuff being bored.

Other expedients may be used. One is to twist a small wire or tie a thread directly around the bit at the proper depth. Another is mark the bit with soapstone or grease pencil, although this is not dependable on a twist bit. Still another way to do it, particularly when one expects to duplicate holes for a long period, is to mark the bit with a small file cut. The wire, however, is the most convenient and the most accurate.

Craftsmen, such as wainwrights, chairmakers and gunstockers, seemed to develop remarkable instincts in gauging and executing holes to a precise angle, either a 90° angle or any other down to 180°. But until such intuition is developed such angles may be controlled in a number of different ways, some almost mechanical in nature.

Every workshop, as with any other building, is filled with various angular shapes: the edges of the workbench which run horizontally, the sides of cabinets or door or window frames which are vertical, perhaps corner braces which are usually at a 45° angle to the floor. When one is working outdoors he can usually find the same angles in buildings some distance away.

Old time woodworkers, always expedient and alert to anything useful, often used these objects as a gauge for sighting the horizontal or vertical positions of bits. After the bit has penetrated the stuff for perhaps a quarter inch the craftsman sights across its axis from the side and matches the line of the axis with the line of a bench top, if he is boring horizontally, or the jamb of a door frame if he is boring vertically. This controls the direction of the hole in one direction. For control in the other direction the bit is sighted along the edge of the board.

Once the bit is perpendicular to the board the workman continues to turn brace or auger but checks his angles several times until the bit has penetrated enough in the stuff to have created a guiding channel. The job of boring a straight hole

Sighting along edge of board

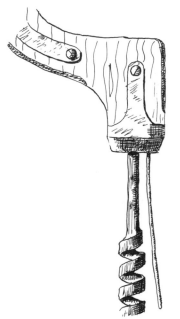

Wire depth gauge

with a brace and bit is made much easier if the worker places his stuff in the vise or on the bench so that the head of the brace is fixed comfortably against chest or shoulder and unlikely to change its predetermined angle because of shifts in body position. A comfortable position offers fine insurance against inaccuracy.

Boring holes at an angle is a different matter, sometimes requiring sighting, sometimes a simple mechanical device and sometimes even an extra pair of eyes.

For long slanted holes, six inches or more in length, as through the cheeks of a naval cannon carriage, if one becomes involved in making a naval cannon carriage, a sighting mark may be used. The angle of the hole is carefully marked with bevel and scribe on the side of the board. After the point of the bit is precisely placed its shank is sighted along this mark, for the angle, and along the edge of the board for perpendicularity in the other direction, then bored in. As always, until the hole is a couple of inches deep to serve as a channel, the position of the bit must be checked every couple of turns to see that its angle remains true. It is helpful when boring long slanted holes to have a second person standing by to check the bit in all directions and correct its angle before it penetrates too deeply into the wood. Once the bit has bored for a couple of inches it is almost impossible to change its direction and correct its angle. If it is not too far in, a long bit may be pulled gently toward the worker to bring the angle toward him or pushed to move the angle away from him. In effect, however, this tends to make a slightly curved hole which will begin to bind the bit after a few turns. Binding can be alleviated by lubricating the bit with linseed oil, dry soap or wax.

If no correction can be effected in the angle, the only solution is to plug the hole already begun and start over with more care. If the new hole is started precisely in the center of the plug the correction will be quite invisible. Care should be taken to see that the plug fits tigthly but is not cut so large that it splits the board when driven in with a mallet.

Still another method of controlling the angle of a hole, particularly for six inches or less where a sighting line might be rather short, is to use a jig. One makes a jig by boring a hole perpendicularly through a piece of stuff two or three inches thick and as wide as the hole requires. The accuracy of the right angle is not overly important because after the hole is bored through, a line is scribed on the outside of the board exactly parallel to the axis of the hole. This line is then bisected by another line to which the first forms the intended angle of the finished hole. The jig is then planed or sawed along this second line so that when the new surface rests on another board the angle of the hole is immutably related to the other board.

Before being used, the jig should have lines scribed parallel to the axis of the hole on both sides and on each end, the end lines corresponding to the center of the hole at top and bottom of the jig. The hole to be bored should have its center marked by two long lines which intersect at right angles. When the lines on the ends and sides of the jig are placed to continue the lines marking the center of the intended hole, then the jig is in proper position and may be secured with clamps or small nails partially driven in.

Jigs may be modified to fit different conditions. For instance, when using a jig on the edge of a board it might be easier to

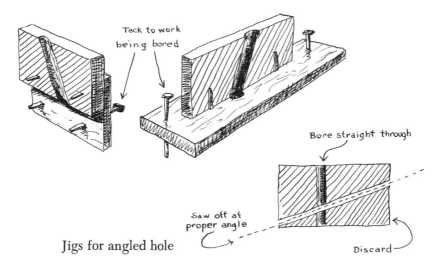

Tack to work being bored

Bore straight through

Saw off at proper angle

Jigs for angled hole

Discard

attach the jig by tacking to its side a thin board which encloses the corner of the edge and may be secured by a clamp placed over the thinner dimension of the stuff to be bored. In other instances a thin board may be applied to the bottom of the jig, its ends extending several inches beyond the ends of the jig itself, again to provide even surfaces which may be more easily clamped than angled surfaces.

It must be pointed out that the makers of Windsor chairs, wagons, benches and other items of wood, usually bored angled holes without benefit of jig or sighting line, relying entirely on instinct and experience. Experience or, more accurately, experience in error, is the essence of such virtuosity in boring. The worker without his seven steady years of apprenticeship should feel no shame in using a jig.

It should be plain that each sized bit requires its own jig and that jigs may be used time and time again, sometimes being altered to fit a new angle, it being easier to modify an old jig than to make a new one. Also, it should be remembered that jigs may only be used for the types of bits with long blades, the shell, the spoon and the twist. Jigs are useless for center bits, diamond bits and pod bits.

As with all hand tools, proper maintenance of boring tools contributes greatly to efficiency and pleasure. The wooden parts of augers, braces and drills should be stored in a dry spot safe from the ravages of rot and powder beetles. Maintaining a coat of varnish helps greatly in protecting the wood from dampness which leads both to rot and to swelling, but wax or boiled linseed oil applied periodically offers equal protection. Components of iron and steel should always be coated lightly with oil, and moving parts should be kept lubricated to minimize wear. Lubrication for wood against wood, as in the knobs of braces and bow drills, should consist of a light application of candle wax or dry soap or, when available, tallow.

Sharpening is the most important aspect of maintenance, and the most frequently repeated. It should not be overdone to the point of wearing down the cutting edges of bits unnecessarily but it should be done often enough so that only a slight touching-up of the edge is necessary. Each of the bits described in this chapter requires different sharpening tools and techniques.

Spoon bits and shell bits must be sharpened with a round, or round-edged, stone of the type known as a slip. These bits must be sharpened on the inside of the bit to maintain the cutting edge on the outside surface, otherwise they will be made useless. With a well-tempered bit only a little stoning with a rotary motion is necessary. Oil applied to the stone will keep the texture free from minuscule particles of steel.

Pod bits must be sharpened on the edges of the twist with either a flat stone or a small finely cut file. Bits are turned in a clockwise direction, requiring that the right corner of the edge of the twist be kept sharp. When filing, this corner should be shaped to about a 60° angle, not exactly a cutting edge but an efficient scraping edge.

Diamond bits used in pump and bow drills must be sharpened to an obtuse knife edge on the bottom side of the diamond to create a 30° angle. Either stone or file may be used.

Center bits must have the cutter and the scriber sharpened with file or stone. Because of the corner created by the cutter and bit head the cutter must be filed lengthwise instead of away from the edge as is common with other cutting surfaces. Care should be taken not to cut into the center point and head when filing the cutter. The edge should be shaped to about 30°.

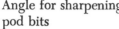

Angle for sharpening
pod bits

Sharpening angle for diamond bit

(File)

Sharpening twist bit

Sharpening center bit

The scriber should be merely touched up with a file to maintain a cutting knife edge on its end.

Only the twist bits do a good job of cutting a hole outlined by the knife-edged scribers which extend below each cutter of the bit. These scribers may be sharpened easily with a couple of passes with the file on each. The bit must be held in a special position to sharpen the cutters. With its screw point set on the bench top, the shank is pushed away from the worker until the edge of the scriber touches the bench with the cutter's edge toward the worker. At this position the cutter edge is filed on the top side to form about a 60° cutting edge. Careful filers will grind off both edges of the file before using it to sharpen twist bits, thereby protecting the spindle section around which the twisted blades are wound.

Bits of all sorts are best kept in a drawer or cabinet stuck upright in holes bored into two-inch boards. Extra long bits may be stored by hanging horizontally on a couple of pegs inserted in the cabinet back.

One secret of enjoying the use of somewhat mundane, inartistic tools such as auger and brace and bit is, as with other tools, to develop a rhythm. And with observation of the principles involved, as well as the differences in each piece of wood being worked, even a boring tool will become interesting.

CHAPTER VII

Chiseling

THE USE of the chisel and that concomitant tool of chisels, the mallet, is quite a simple elementary exercise in principle, requiring little explanation and learned quickly through a minimum experience. Perhaps the most important thing to learn about the chisel is the variety of design and function of this simple prehistoric tool, the basic use of each type and the use of the tool in combination with other tools such as the brace and bit and the saw.

There are two main types. The firming or forming chisel is used almost invariably with a wooden mallet, its function being to rough out mortises and occasionally to plane a surface on a component of an already assembled house, coach or piece of furniture. Firmers usually have a rather heavy blade of varying width with a basiled edge. Most have wooden handles which are fitted into a conical socket joined on the opposite end of the blade from the edge, although a few older types have a tang formed with a supporting collar adjacent to the blade, which is inserted into a wooden handle. A few examples of homemade firming chisels are of all steel including the handle. Firming chisels are designed to be struck with a wooden mallet, if the chisel handle is of wood, or with a regular steel-headed hammer if of metal.

The other basic type of chisel is called a paring chisel. In appearance it resembles the firmer but is quite different in having a slimmer blade, invariably tanged and with a wooden handle and always with a knife edge sharpened on both sides.

Firmer blade and basil
Paring chisel

Mortising ax in use

In effect, paring chisels are knives rather than chisels. They are never struck with the mallet but are pushed, as the name suggests, to pare rough surfaces, such as the inside of mortises which have been earlier formed by firming chisel and mallet. Like firmers, paring chisels come in varying widths.

Both firmers and paring chisels have survived the onslaught of the machine age and are almost indispensable in certain types of modern woodwork. There are other types of chisels, however, which were common in earlier days but which have disappeared from the modern scene. Most of these may be called "set" chisels, to borrow a term from the blacksmith, in that the blades are fitted with wooden handles perpendicular to the long axis of the blade. Indeed, they resemble axes more than regular chisels, but most are struck with mallet, maul or hammer when used. Though considered members of the firmer family, some set chisels have a knife edge and can be used for paring as well as forming. The twivel is an exception in that it is used for paring and is never struck.

The mortising ax actually resembles an ax, having a heavy head with a poll and a knife edge, but differing in that its bit is elongated and tapered. It is used mostly for very heavy work in forming mortises in fence posts and heavy building timbers. To use it one places the edge on a mortise half formed with bored holes and strikes the poll with a heavy wooden mallet.

A twybil is actually two chisels joined at the base with a long-handle socket at right angles to the point of junction. The edges are deeply basiled, one being parallel to the axis of the handle, the other being perpendicular to the handle. Used to cut large mortises in forming timbers, the twybil is sometimes swung and sometimes driven by striking with a heavy mallet on the long handle-socket. The edges, perpendicular to each other, allow the workman to use this tool to form both sides and ends of a mortise by merely reversing the edges with no change of position required.

Twivels are two-bladed affairs with a socketed handle at right angles to the head, but the blades are formed into a small hook at each end of the curved head and the hooks are sharpened to a knife edge on the bottom. It is used by grasping the handle with one hand and blade with the other to pare the sides of a mortise with a pulling or gentle chopping motion.

While mallets seem to be dull unimaginative tools quite unworthy of any attention, the master woodworker knows the

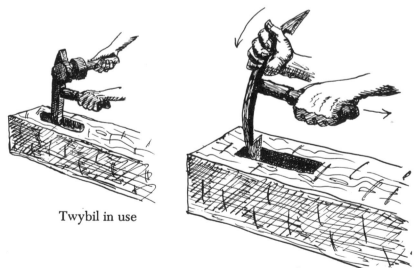

Twybil in use

Twivel in use

value of having several, of different weights and designs, in the shop as part and parcel of his set of firming chisels. For, as with any other striking tool, the weight of the mallet provides a measure of control over the cut of the chisel in relation both to the size of the chisel and to the type wood being worked.

Light mallets are easily made in any shop. Any type of hard, close-grained wood is suitable for the head, and handles are usually of hickory. Sometimes the heads are turned on the lathe to a perfect cylinder but more often than not the heads are a section of a limb or sapling of dogwood, beech, hornbeam or hickory, with a hole bored in the center and a handle inserted and wedged. When possible, the head is cut when the wood is green so that its natural shrinkage as it dries will bond green head and dry handle together as though the two pieces had grown that way.

Another type mallet frequently illustrated in old art and prints from the thirteenth to the nineteenth centuries is a small refined version of the maul used to split logs and shingles. In this type the roughly cylindrical head and handle are turned from one piece of beech, hornbeam (or ironwood), boxwood, lignum vitae or other hard, close-grained wood. Sizes range from two inches to four or five inches in diameter. Such

Three types of mallets

mallets are still available in the 1970s in art supply shops which cater to wood sculptors. They are well balanced and a pleasure to use with chisels. The versatile woodworker should have about three of them of various weights which fit his strength, his set of chisels and the type work he intends to do.

A third type mallet has a head resembling a short, thick felloe of a wheel rim with a handle inserted in the radius of the arc. The eye, through which the handle is inserted, is tapered from the outside of the arc inward so that a tapered handle may be inserted from the outside and jambed in position by centrifugal force when the mallet is in use. The heads of arched mallets are made of hard close-grained wood and the handles made of ash or hickory, the latter being perferred. This type mallet is generally rather heavy and is used for heavy work with large chisels such as mortising house or bridge timbers.

A set of four or five firming, or forming, chisels and two or three paring chisels, with several mallets of different weights, will suffice the average woodworker for building houses or simple furniture. The craftsman of yore who made his living building or joining, however, would also own some specialized chisels, mainly gouges, and a thick, deeply basiled mortising chisel or two. Many would also own a corner chisel which saves many blows in forming good, square corners in house or barn mortises. Many, too, might have owned a slick, that giant paring chisel up to three feet in overall length, with an edge three to four inches wide, which was pushed from the shoulder to pare the irregularities from floor joists or wall timbers.

However simple the design of a firming chisel may seem, an examination and analysis of its elements, particularly the deeply basiled edge, will indicate the necessity of special techniques in its use, particularly in cutting apertures such as mortises. It becomes apparent from examination that the 30° basil of the edge not only cuts but also exerts a wedging action whenever it penetrates the wood, thereby affecting the direction of the cut. A perpendicular cross-grain cut, as in the end of a mortise, will force the straight side of the chisel backward because of the wedging action of wood against basil. If the position of the chisel is reversed so that the basil is next to the mark with

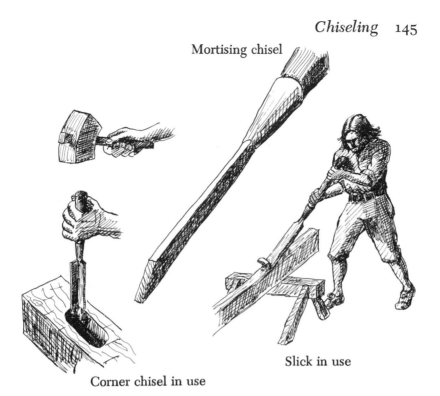

Mortising chisel

Corner chisel in use

Slick in use

the edge of the basil held vertically, then the cut slants in the opposite direction.

Since it is the bulk of wood to be removed which controls this wedging action, a mortise or other opening should be started by chiseling out the center of the portion of wood to be removed with a series of shallow V-shaped cuts. To do this the chisel is held with the basiled side of the edge down, the plane of the basil being at almost 50° to the top surface of the stuff being worked. The chisel is then tapped in with a mallet of proper weight for chisel and hardness of wood to about a quarter inch depth. It is then removed and cut in at the same angle and depth from the opposite direction. After the second cut, the chisel is left in place and its handle pushed downward to allow the angle of basil, where it meets the straight line of the blade, to act as a fulcrum so that the chip can be levered out of the beginning recess. Once the chip is removed the process is repeated with the chisel being held at progressively sharper angles until the intended depth of the recess has been reached. At

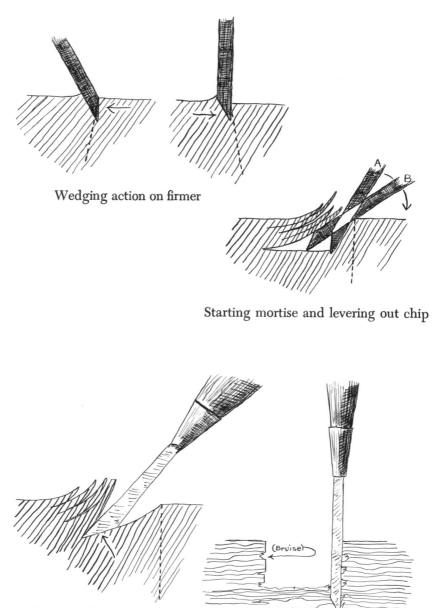

Wedging action on firmer

Starting mortise and levering out chip

Mortising chisel in use

Chisel and bruising

this time the ends of the mortise are dressed by driving the chisel with light strokes until the inside surfaces of the ends are nearly perpendicular to the surface of the shift.

Absolute, or as near absolute as possible, perpendicularity is achieved by paring. For this a paring chisel, without mallet, may be used or the firmer chisel may be honed to razor sharpness and used as a paring chisel, the flat side of the edge being placed next to the mortise end so that the flat length of the blade may guide the cutting.

In cutting large mortises in heavy stuff, such as house or barn timbers, the mortising chisel comes into use. It is used exactly as the firmer is on small mortises. Its thicker blade and consequently longer basil increase the wedging power of the edge and expedite the removal of wood. The mortising chisel requires a rather heavy mallet and it may be driven in as deeply as an inch or more before prising out the chip.

After cutting, the sides of a mortise as well as the ends should be pared smooth with a paring or a firming chisel to insure as tight a fit as possible with the tenon and to offer as tight bonding with glue as possible in mortised and tenoned joints of furniture.

Those workers who will cut mortises in soft woods such as pine, spruce and fir, should be cautioned always to use a very sharp chisel when cutting across grain to form the end of a recess. Otherwise the end grain of soft stuff will be bruised; that is, portions of the grain will break and detach themselves from the end leaving a pitted surface which adversely affects fit and bonding. Sometimes in soft woods the worker will eschew the use of the mallet to form the ends of a mortise using only a sharp firmer or paring chisel.

For large mortises in large timbers of soft wood the worker will find it to his advantage to grind his firmer edge askew. This means that the cutting edge not only is basiled but is also ground askew at an angle of from 15° to 30° to the thin edge of the blade. Skew edges on chisels eliminate much of the problem of bruising.

While there may be purists in chisel techniques most craftsmen of older times were pragmatists with no compunctions against using the combination of tools which made the job of

Firmer clearing housed joint mortise

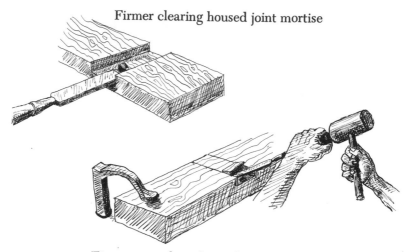

Firmer smoothing housed joint mortise

forming mortises easiest. Accordingly, most mortises in furniture or buildings may have most of the wood removed with auger or brace and bit. The chisel is then used to dress the roughly formed cavity to its intended dimensions, with paring alone on small mortises.

On large mortises the corner chisel may be used as a firmer to cut exact corners in the mortise. These usually large chisels may have the edge basiled on either the inside or the outside of the 90° angle of the blade. Since corner chisels cannot be reversed as with flat firmers, one must be careful to consider the effect of wedging action or the direction of cut and hold the chisel accordingly when the mortise corner is dressed to perfection.

Housed joints, which are open-end mortises cut across grain on a board to receive the butt of shelves or stair treads, also require the use of the firmer chisel for removing wood and dressing inside surfaces. The sides of housed joints are most easily cut with rabbet or backsaw. The wood between the saw cuts is then removed with firmer and mallet, the firmer being held with its basil upward to wedge out the crossgrain wood. Dressing is done also with a firmer held in the same position and pushed across grain through the roughly finished channel to remove irregularities from the bottom of the joint. Here again, since crossgrain wood is being shaped, a skew-edged chisel is a bit more efficient than the straight edge, but certainly it is not essential.

Occasionally in house or furniture construction a deep recess is split out between two saw cuts for some joint. For recesses more than four inches long several saw cuts are made. The chisel is used to split out the waste, being pounded in with the grain until the block pops out. Since there is no room to employ a plane or drawknife, to smooth the bottom of the recess, a chisel must be used to pare the splintery bottom to finished smoothness. Usually a firmer, sharpened to a razor's edge, is used for this paring, it being pushed with the grain or across the grain, depending on circumstances, with basil down, until the surface is smooth and level.

Dovetailing also requires a chisel. Male dovetails are first cut carefully with the dovetail saw, but the excess wood between the dovetails must be removed carefully with a small firmer chisel. The technique used is exactly that of cutting the end of a mortise. First the board is placed on top of another thin board, to protect the top of the workbench, both being secured with a holdfast or clamp. Then a narrow firmer and light mallet are employed with care being taken on the final paring to assure an almost invisible joint.

Female dovetails, almost always found in the end grain, also

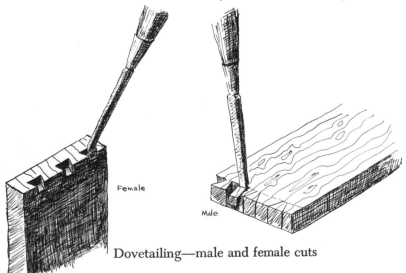

Female

Male

Dovetailing—male and female cuts

require the use of a chisel. For this work the stuff is usually secured in a front vise, the openings toward the worker. After sawing the sides of the dovetail recesses with the dovetail saw, a diagonal cut, the firmer is used to cut out the recess. First the line on the end grain is cut, as with a mortise, then the side is chiseled out. As the saw cut does not reach the back lower corners of the recess, the chisel is used to shape these carefully, roughly with the firmer and mallet, then pared to final dimensions. For small dovetails the worker may prefer to use only a very sharp paring chisel for the whole job.

There are times in the life of a woodworker when cross-grained wood of obstinate character must be pared smooth and the ideal tool needed for the job, a skew-edged chisel, is not available. In such cases one must rely on expedience. He uses a straight edged paring chisel or firmer and pushes it on a line askew from the chisel edge. To do so he pushes, as usual, with his right hand on the handle, but the direction of effort is not along the axis of the chisel blade but on a line some 60° off this axis. The blade is steadied in its angular position by the fingers of the left hand which press the blade down on the stuff being pared.

Experience will show that using the fingers of the left hand to steady and press down the chisel blade is indeed an effective technique for any paring, straight or askew.

Whenever the edge of a board must be planed with a chisel for one reason or another, the edge of the chisel would always be wider than the board. Otherwise it is almost certain that the corners of the edge will score the surface, requiring an onerous stint of rasping and sanding to bring the surface to its intended plane.

Gouges are used both as firmers and as paring chisels. Like chisels, gouges are found with edges from one eighth to two inch width and, in addition, are made with eight different degrees of curve, from a very shallow curve described as very flat, to a full half circle described as a fluting curve. Paring gouges have a knife edge and are better known in small sizes as woodcarving tools. Firming gouges, with socketed handles, have basiled edges.

Many carpenters and some cabinetmakers might live a full career without ever using a gouge. In certain instances, however,

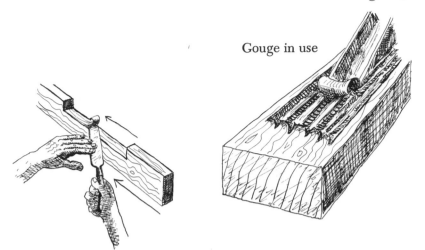

Gouge in use

Pushing straight-edge chisel askew

gouges are necessary to make certain forms, and they are more efficient than flat-edged chisels for removing an excess of wood. Of course, a gouge is necessary to rough cut fluting in a Doric or Grecian porch column and similar forms, the fluting sometimes being done completely with the gouge and then sanded, sometimes being roughed out with the gouge and planed with a plow molding plane of proper size.

The most common variation of the gouge is called a goose-neck because of the double crook given the blade near its end which resembles the neckline of an angry goose. This type is used for hollowing bowls or dugouts or other items with a deep depression and, in centuries past, was found mostly in the shop of the now extinct, and almost forgotten, white cooper, a special-ist in small containers made of wood. Without its curved blade the white cooper could never have properly carved the bottom of a dough bowl. Musical instrument makers still use small-sized gooseneck gouges to rough out the inside of violin, cello, viola and bass violin backs and bellies. Very small gooseneck gouges are found in every complete set of woodcarving tools.

Regardless of the type, every gouge cuts with the grain and never across grain. As with chisels, some gouges are used with mallets, others purely as paring tools.

No chisel, firmer or paring, can be used effectively or with pleasure unless it is kept sharp. A heavy mallet might drive a

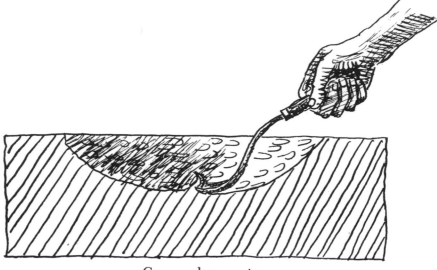

Gooseneck gouge in use

dull chisel along its miserable way but a sharp edge is essential
for the delicacy of true workmanship and the satisfaction of
artistic attainment. A sharp edge reflects professional attitude
and aspiration.

Sharpening chisels is not difficult if the edge is maintained
by adequate stoning and honing. There is no standard which
dictates how frequently the edge must be touched up on the
stone, but it is a good idea to give it a few strokes on the stone
at the outset of every job. If soft pine is being worked a chisel
edge will hold up for hours without need for additional dressing
unless the wood contains an excess of knots. The harder the
wood the more frequently the edge of the chisel must be stoned.

Sharpening requires some care in maintaining a stable position of the chisel edge while moving it about the face of the
stone. The edge should be held so that the basil of a firmer
chisel or the edge-angle of a paring chisel is about 1° or 2°
to the face of the stone. Taking care to keep the surface of basil
in position, the chisel may be moved either in a small circle or
in a figure eight some fifteen or twenty times on the stone. If
a firmer chisel is being sharpened, the blade is reversed so that
the flat side of the edge is flat on the stone, then it is pushed forward gently three or four times to remove any wire edge. For

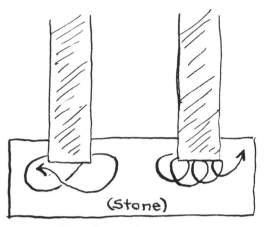

Two sharpening movements

paring chisels each side of the edge is sharpened the same way, but after the second side has been stoned the blade is reversed and pushed forward, as with the firmer, to remove the wire edge.

After stoning, chisels should be honed on a very hard, very fine grained honing stone, the same process being used as in stoning. Honing is followed by stropping the edge about ten times in the palm of the hand. This is done by drawing the edge backward through the palm of the hand while pressing it downward. The blade of the chisel should be held almost parallel to the palm.

Gouges are sharpened in practically the same manner except that the curve basil must be rotated so that every part of the surface is stoned, requiring many times more circular or figure eight movements than for a flat chisel. And, once the gouge is concave on the inside, the wire edge must be removed with a curved slip, a coarse slip being used for initial sharpening and a honing slip being used for honing. Slips are stones which are triangular in section but with base and apex rounded to fit different sized curves.

Chisels must be held steadily with the edge exactly parallel to the face of the stone during the whole of the sharpening movement. Otherwise the corners of the edge will be ground

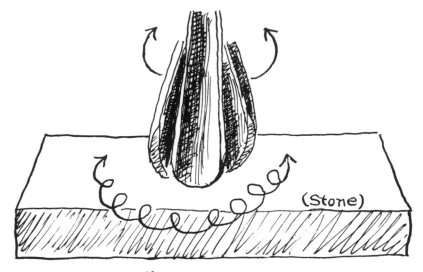

Sharpening the gouge

down before the center resulting in a curved edge, or one side will be ground down resulting in a skew edge. Neither condition will allow the chisel to be used properly. The same thing can happen to a gouge with adverse effect on the efficiency of the tool.

Such mishaps may be corrected by dressing the edge with either a small, flat mill bastard file or a hand-turned grindstone. After grinding, the edge should be dressed to razor sharpness by stoning and honing.

The efficiency of stones and hones is greatly increased by applying a few drops of lubricating oil on the surface before using. Oil does not lubricate but it penetrates the almost invisible pores of the stone and washes out the infinitesimal grains of steel which result from sharpening. If these small particles are not removed the stone will become clogged and unable to perform its grinding function.

Chiseling and gouging are not difficult operations in hand woodworking but they do require technique, often individual, which is developed with experience. The main thing to be remembered is that chisels and gouges are cutting tools and no amount of strength of the power of a heavy mallet will replace the efficiency, and pleasure, which stems from a sharp edge.

CHAPTER VIII

Shaping

Two TOOLS similar in the techniques of use and design and almost identical in function are used to shape smaller timbers and boards and provide a smooth, if somewhat irregular, surface. These are the drawknife and the spokeshave, both already unfamiliar to many modern woodworkers and somewhat difficult to acquire in modern stores. Some varieties of these two old tools, once common in the shops of coopers, wheelwrights and other old-time craftsmen, have gone out of use with the crafts which used them and are now categorically classified as antiques

Another old tool, the block knife, has been relegated to oblivion, except in Europe, for some time now, and has been replaced by power routers and jig saws and saber saws to shape irregular items such as clog soles and the outsides of dough bowls. Yet the block knife does an efficient, precise job of shaping wood, offering the ancient mechanical advantage of leverage to hand carving.

And of course, there is the knife, still common and still useful to different degrees with woodworkers ranging from whittlers to sculptors. The knife is made in so many forms and its techniques of use are so basic that it may be dismissed, with honor, by saying that its edge should always be kept sharp and turned away from the woodworker, and that a knife should be present among the tools of any worker of wood.

Drawknives, or drawing knives, have changed practically not at all since the appearance of this tool in prehistoric times.

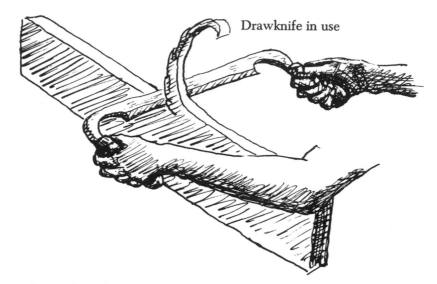

Drawknife in use

It has a thick blade from eight inches to a foot long with a tang at each end which is bent at a 90° angle to the blade on the same plane as the blade. Each tang is inserted into a turned wooden handle which is secured by clinching or bradding the tang over the end of the handle. The edge is deeply basiled and kept razor sharp, making the tool resemble an elongated firming chisel edge, although the drawknife is never struck by mallet or hammer. Unlike most of the cutting tools for wood, it is usually pulled or drawn toward the worker to pare off thin or thick slices of wood in the direction of the grain.

Most craftsmen use the tool with its basiled edge down to allow its edge to penetrate the wood being worked. The blade is used to cut from barely beneath the surface of the wood, to produce a shaving of paper thinness, to a full inch on soft woods. The depth of the cut is controlled by the degree of rotation given the handles. For a deep curve the handles might be rotated through wrist action to a full 60°; for long level cuts of little depth the handles are held steadily at the same relative angle to the surface of the wood, the control being maintained by the wrists.

Some users of the drawknife prefer to hold the tool with its basil upward while making a level cut, the flat side of the blade serving as a guide to help keep the cut on one intended plane.

For deep curved cuts, however, the blade should be reversed with basil down, as the angular surface on the basiled side of the blade lends itself better to a curved surface. Basil up or basil down is really a matter of individual taste, and neither position should be taken as a matter of dogma. Comfort and control are the standards by which either position must be judged, and judgment must be made by each individual craftsman.

In certain situations, where very delicate shaping must be done with a drawknife, the tool is pushed; again, as a matter of control, the pushing being done entirely with the arms, wrist motion again being used to control the depth and evenness of the cut. This technique, though preferred by some, is uncommon. Drawknives are more effective when drawn toward the worker so that the weight of the body may be utilized to cut away a volume of wood.

Drawknives are not generally used as finishing tools, but to rough out all manner of shapes for components of furniture, tools and buildings. Ax handles, peavy handles and hammer handles are easily roughed out with a drawknife and finished with a spokeshave and scraper. Chair legs and arms and backs, the curved feet of beds and chair rockers are often roughly shaped with the drawknife. Split shingles and clapboards are given a smooth finish with a drawknife.

But the drawknife may often be used for quite mundane tasks which have only an indirect association with fine joining and strong building. Blacksmiths use them to prepare shavings with which to start the fire in the forge. Saplings, cut for hoe or shovel handles, may have the bark removed with a drawknife. Turners who work on pole or treadle wood lathes will round the corners of square wooden timbers with the drawknife to save time and effort at the lathe.

Also, the cooper and the white cooper, of now lamented memory, used specially formed drawknives to shape the concave insides of barrel staves and to finish the insides of bowls which had been roughed out with gooseneck gouges or gouge adzes.

A cooper's drawknife, as might be expected, has a curved rather than a flat blade but with the same two handles driven into tangs at both ends. Some cooper's drawknives have both

Cooper's drawknife

Uses of cooper's drawknife in shaping inside and outside of barrel staves

a curved and a flat section in the blade so that the craftsman can use one tool to hollow the stave, to shape its convex outside with the blade reversed, and to trim its edge with the straight section of the blade.

The white cooper used a modified form of the drawknife, called a scorp or scoop, to finish the spherical insides of wooden bowls. Scorps generally consist of a ring of steel with one tang onto which a handle is driven. This type is pulled with one hand. Another type has an almost circular blade with two handles, making it an exaggerated form of the more gently curved cooper's drawknife.

Most stuff being worked with a drawknife must be secured in a vise or with a clamp of some sort, since the two-handed tool makes it quite impossible for a craftsman to use it and hold the stuff at the same time.

The best device to hold shingles and tool handles while being shaped is the shaving horse, a massive affair of boards and logs only vaguely resembling a horse. Actually it is a heavy plank or puncheon some six feet long with three or four peg legs, and an attached angled surface through which a pivoting clamp is fastened with a stout peg. The clamp is no more than a section of log carved to provide it with a boss on one end and a long stake which may be pushed by the seated worker's foot to secure a shingle or ax handle between clamp head and angled surface. Some refined versions have an upright spring of hickory inserted in the horse behind the clamp and fastened to the clamp head, to release the work automatically when pressure from the foot is removed.

Spokeshaves, unfamiliar to most people born since 1940, are pull tools like the drawknife, but with the advantage of a short sole through which the adjustable blade protrudes to give this tool the control of depth found in planes. Older versions have a wooden stock with a handle on each side which is parallel to the blade. Since about 1900, though, most spokeshaves have been manufactured with a stock of cast iron.

In earlier spokeshaves the short narrow blade had a tang at each end which is bent at a 90° angle to the plane of the blade and inserted through two holes in the stock. The tangs fit rather tightly in the holes to provide enough friction to hold the blade at any desired distance from the sole, thereby controlling the depth of cut. Later types with wooden stocks had the tangs threaded and engaged in two fixed nuts so that delicate adjustments for depth could be made by turning the nuts.

Virtually all spokeshaves with cast iron stocks are designed with a shallow throat, as on a plane, and are equipped with a short plane-type blade and a cap iron, to break and facilitate the removal of shavings through the throat. Depth of the blade

Two handled scorp

One handled scorp

Shaving horse

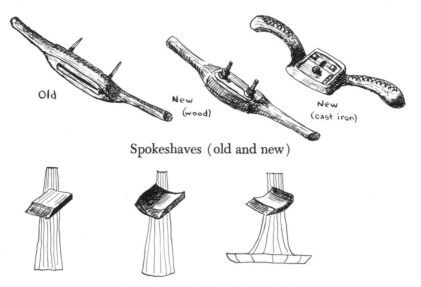

Old   New (wood)   New (cast iron)

Spokeshaves (old and new)

Three forms of spokeshave blades

is adjusted on this newer form by two fixed screws, one on each side of the blade, engaged in free-moving knurled nuts which fit into two notches in the blade. The blade is fixed to the stock with a screw which passes through a slot. To adjust, the screw is loosened and the knurled knots are turned as desired to fix the intended depth of the blade as well as to adjust the angle of the edge.

While most spokeshaves have a straight blade, some are found with a curved blade, as is the cooper's drawknife, and some have straight edges with the blade curving back from the edge to allow precise finishing of rounded inside corners.

As the name suggests, the spokeshave probably originated in the wheelwright's shop where it was invented to shape carefully and to smooth the spokes of wagon and carriage wheels. It was soon adopted, however, by master carpenters, cabinetmakers and white coopers. It is used in the manner of a refined drawknife.

There is also a form of scorp which employs the principle of spokeshave design. It has a heavy wooden stock with an integrated handle carved on top. Its blade is curved with a vertical tang on each end. Tangs are inserted through holes in the stock, exactly as with the earlier spokeshaves, so that the depth of the

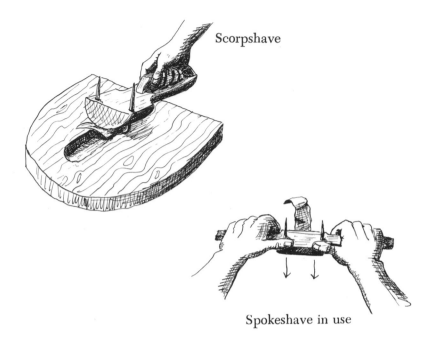

Scorpshave

Spokeshave in use

blade can be easily adjusted. Scorpshaves such as this are most
efficient in dressing the insides of wooden bowls.

All forms of spokeshaves offer great pleasure and satisfaction in use. When the blade is sharp, as it should be always, the
weight of the body pulling it along the wood makes the operation seem effortless; yet, as if by magic, the long shaving coils
from the throat, like a thing alive, pristine, clean and fragrant,
leaving behind the moving tool a smooth surface never before
seen by human eye. This satisfaction only occurs if the spokeshave is held steadily, clamped in position by the wrists, as it
were, keeping the sole as nearly as possible on an even plane
regardless of original minor irregularities in the surface being
shaved, The blade should never be set too deep, for the spokeshave is for shaving; deep cuts should be made with the drawknife. Minimum experience will teach the spokeshaver that a
mild downward pressure on the front edge of the sole, controlled
by the wrists of course, will do much to keep the sole level as
the tool is pulled.

Block knives, in several different forms, are mostly inherited from certain woodworking specialists such as clog sole makers, sabot makers and in some instances chair makers and wooden bowl makers. The most common form of the tool consists of a knife blade from one to two feet long with a hooked tang forged on one end and a straight tang, which is inserted into a wooden handle, on the other end. Sometimes the handle is straight, parallel with the blade, and sometimes it takes the form of a T handle, the tang piercing it in the middle and clinched.

There are modifications to the long blade, however. Some block knives have a knife edge and some a basiled edge like the drawknife. And some have a chisel blade welded at a right angle to the middle of a two foot long bar with hook and handle. This chisel is sometimes straight and sometimes curved to make it easier to carve out the inside of an object such as a bowl or a sabot. To provide more variety of movement, chisel block knives are sometimes given a slight curve in the long bar.

A basic part of this tool is the block which gives it its name. Usually a section of tree trunk about two feet in diameter, the block, as with any good tool, stands at a height to fit the worker, usually to reach the knuckles of his hand when he stands upright with arms by his side. At one corner of the block is a stout

Chisel knife

Block knife in use

Height of block

staple driven deeply into the wood in which the hook on the end of the blade is engaged. Assembled, the block knife becomes an edged lever or a levered chisel providing the Archimedean advantage of levered power to the weight and strength of body and arms.

To use the block knife one holds the stuff he is shaping on the block with its direction of grain upright and grasps the handle of the knife with his right hand. The knife is lifted and applied to the wood, then levered downard to slice as desired.

Despite the fixed relationship of knife and block, great flexibility is available in the use of this tool. Coupling of hook and staple is so loose that the blade can be rotated a full 180° and held in position for straight cuts or rotated in action for curved cuts. In addition, the stuff being shaped can also be turned in any direction, vertically or horizontally, while the cut is being made. With both stuff and knife moving, the block knife is capable of extreme versatility. The advantage of leverage, which varies according to how closely the stuff is placed at the fulcrum point of hook and staple, offers great force with little effort and good control with which to effect quite delicate shaping. With the slightly curved bar on some chisel-type block knives even greater movement is possible, ideal for scooping out cavities of one sort or another.

Shaping tools are all sharpened with stone and hone. Drawknives are held by one handle, the other resting on the workbench top so that the blade is held diagonally to the bench, making it easy to stone and hone with a circular or figure eight movement. Of course, the stone is moved and the tool held in a stationary position. The original plane of the basil must be maintained carefully while sharpening.

Old type spokeshaves are sharpened by removing the blade and holding it by one tang on the bench top so that it leans slightly away from the worker, then using small stones and hones to sharpen its edge. Care should be taken to maintain a straight edge. Newer types with plane blade must also have the blade removed for sharpening. The blade, with cap iron either removed or left in place, is held in a steady relationship to the stone and rubbed on the stone in a circular or figure eight movement exactly as when sharpening a firming chisel edge.

Sharpening drawknife

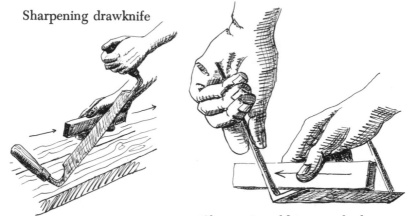

Sharpening old type spokeshave

Block knives are detached from the staple in the block and sharpened in the same manner as drawknives. Knife-edged block knives can also be sharpened on an old fashioned grindstone.

As with other tools, shaping tools should be protected against rust by coating the metal parts lightly with oil and rubbing boiled linseed oil into the wooden components.

Properly maintained and kept sharp, drawknife, spokeshave and block knife are valuable tools for any handcraftsman in wood.

CHAPTER IX

Planing

IF EVER an object must be chosen to symbolize the height of craftsmanship in woodworking it will probably be the plane. A number of other tools require more skill and talent to use, among them the simple ax, and felling a tree properly reflects far more experience than planing a board. But no other tool offers the esthetic qualities of fine molding, inlay and joining which are produced by the plane.

Although the planes of olden days are found in infinite variety for many special types of work, all are made and used alike in principle. The old style wooden stocked plane is itself a thing of beauty, esthetically and functionally, its stock polished with use, its form well proportioned and logical, its work satisfying. Like most tools the plane has been modified and improved for about a century and is still commonly available in most hardware stores, but as a category it has suffered in the process of change and improvement. Planes offered in the 1970s are limited to about a dozen different kinds, and most are made with cast iron stocks which simply are not as pretty as stocks of beech and hornbeam, lignum vitae and rosewood. Wooden stocked planes are still made and used in Europe, but the variety of olden times is lacking. Since there are in existence some excellent books which cover the use and care of modern planes, this chapter will deal only with the classic planes with wooden stocks which were used universally by many types of woodworkers before 1860.

All planes follow basically the same design. Each is made

of a block of wood which has an opening chiseled through it to receive a blade, set at an angle, and a wooden wedge to secure the blade in position. Each has a throat through which the shavings are ejected as the tool is pushed along the stuff. The differences between various types are minor and often superficial.

In the Western world almost all planes are pushed along the wood; in the Orient most are pulled, but this is a difference in technique rather than functional design.

There are three broad categories into which planes may be classified. The first is made up of smoothing planes, those used to smooth a flat surface by removing saw or adz marks from a board to create a mechanically perfect plane, hence the name.

The second and most numerous group consists of molding planes which do not create a plane at all but carve, alone or in combination, beautiful moldings for decorative effect. It is the molding planes which provide the woodworker with a source of artistic achievement which sometimes approaches sculpture.

Rabbetting planes, including moving fillisters, comprise the last broad category. While sometimes used as auxiliary planes in carving molding, the rabbetting planes are generally tools for joining boards together or for allowing other materials such as glass to be fitted precisely into wooden frames. Some rabbetting planes, especially those made from the latter part of the eighteenth century to 1900, are equipped with brass depth gauges which precisely control the depth of the cut. Moving fillisters are planes equipped not only with depth gauges but also with adjustable fences which are attached to the plane by threaded or wedged arms that allow the fence, or side guide, to be set to control the distance of the cut from the side of the board. Sets of tongue and groove planes as well as tiny inlay planes are considered rabbetting planes.

Of some interest to etymologists, the word *rabbet* apparently is derived from the old French word *rabetter,* but the meaning of the original word has been lost. In England, these planes are called rebate planes, which has no more meaning than the French word except as an illustration of the typical way the English tongue corrupts foreign words.

Like saw teeth, the angle at which a plane blade is set in

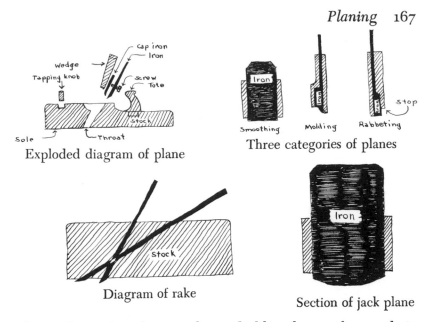

Exploded diagram of plane

Three categories of planes

Diagram of rake

Section of jack plane

the stock is referred to as rake, and older planes, often made in the shop before 1750, show several different rakes for different woods. An all-purpose plane will generally have a rake of 45° from the horizontal, an angle most suitable for planing soft woods. According to Henry Mercer, a rake of 50° does a better job of planing hard or stringy woods, 55° for molding planes on soft wood or smoothing planes for mahogany and 60° for molding planes of mahogany and such difficult woods as birds-eye maple.

The toothing plane has its blade set at 80° to 90° to the sole of the plane, but despite its name it is not a cutting tool. Its generally understood purpose is to scratch furrows in a board preparatory to applying glue and joining veneer to the surface. Recent study by Dr. Frank Allbright of Old Salem Village, however, indicates that toothing planes were also used to remove the wood roughly before employing smoothing planes for final finishing.

Smoothing planes are basic to any woodworker's tool kit and both carpenters and cabinetmakers, as well as wheelwrights, carriage makers, coffin makers and other trades, needed them in olden times.

Possibly the one used most often before the days of planing mills, which originated around 1850, is the jack plane or fore plane, a block about 15″ long with a blade 2½″–3″ wide. Usually it has a closed handle or tote, much like a panel saw handle and sometimes it has an offset surface on the block behind the throat.

The distinguishing feature of the jack plane is the convex edge on its blade, reflecting its specialized use. For this tool is used for rough leveling before a board is smoothed or molded with other planes. Its curved edge, like the curved edge of a felling ax, bites more deeply into the wood with less effort expended and removes long, coarse shavings, leaving characteristic long troughs in the board being worked, but reducing the dimensions of any piece of stuff quickly and efficiently. Examples of jack planing are found on the bottoms of eighteenth century drawers or on the backs of mirrors and wainscoting and in other places that do not show.

The undulation left by the jack plane may be leveled off with the trying, or truing, plane, a tool of from fifteen to twenty inches long, somewhat broader than the jack plane and with an absolutely square edge. This plane is used to shave off high points of the undulations produced by the jack, but leaving a slight indication of the jack planing. If all traces of undulation are removed the corner of the trying plane blade will likely cut angular offsets in the wood, thereby ruining the wavy texture which is so characteristic of hand-planed lumber, and so beautiful.

There is yet another long plane, the joining plane, with a sole up to three feet long, most of it in front of the blade which is set close before the tote with the same relative positions of blade and tote as is found in the jack plane. Its long sole provides a constant level track for the blade as it courses along the edges of long boards preparing them for being joined together in perfect fit. Also known as a flooring plane, this long john may be used to level flooring which has already been laid with wooden pegs. For either task the blade is set shallowly to remove only shavings of paper thinness.

But wood being somewhat obstinate, and with each board being somewhat different from all others, even the mechanically perfect surface of a joining plane will not make the edges of two boards fit perfectly together. This must be done with the smoothing plane, a small plane with no tote, only about eight

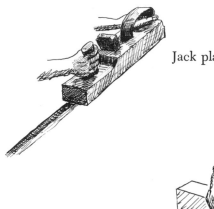

Jack plane in use

Handling the smoothing plane

inches long with curved sides which give it the appearance of a small boat and with the edge of its blade protruding slightly across the midpoint of its sole. It is used to remove slight irregularities left by the joining plane so that two boards can fit together perfectly.

The smoothing plane's function brings to mind the advice of Benjamin Franklin during the Constitutional Convention of 1787. At a time when two factions at the convention were deadlocked over the issue of just representation in Congress, Franklin inspired a workable compromise by observing that if a joiner wished to fit two boards together he had to shave a little from each. In woodworking such compromise is made possible by the smoothing plane.

While the planes described here were all included in the tools of carpenter and cabinetmaker, there are other smoothing planes both larger and smaller which were needed by special woodworkers such as carriage builders, musical instrument makers and coopers.

Carriage builders and musical instrument makers frequently called to use a series of very small, one hand planes known as finger planes. These are no more than small block

Finger plane in use

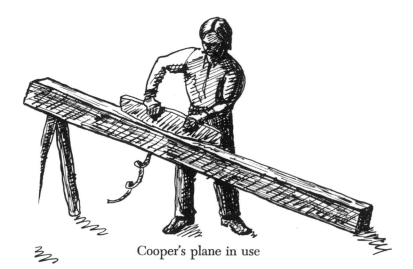

Cooper's plane in use

planes made exactly like the larger ones but with soles only three and four inches long. Some of them have rounded soles for such tasks as smoothing the insides of violin backs and bellies, or rounding the corners of carriage bodies or the dashboards of sleighs.

Coopers used the largest of the smoothing planes, a huge joiner about six feet long, too long and heavy to handle with delicacy on the workbench. Because of its size the cooper's joining plane is reversed in use so that the edge of its blade is uppermost, and it is propped up to waist height on one end with two spread peglegs mortised into the stock, its other end resting on the floor. When using it to trim the arched edges of barrel staves; the cooper holds the stave in his hands and slides its edge over the plane blade, quite the reverse of normal planing technique.

Many wooden-stocked smoothing planes of European provenience, including those still mass-produced in Switzerland, West Germany and other nations in the 1970s, are equipped with a horn, integrally carved into the stock or dovetailed into the forestock. This device provides a handhold for the left hand to make it easier to push, but it is not necessary and is seldom found on old planes of British and American manufacture. The front knob of later American planes with cast iron stocks, however, offers a revived semblance of the horn. Neither horn nor knob changes the basic technique of using the smoothing plane.

A northern European phenomenon of the seventeenth and eighteenth centuries is the elaborately carved smoothing plane, in all sizes with decorations of floral, geometric or grotesque designs, including date of manufacture and owner's initials, all in deep bas relief of sculptural quality. Such carving reflected the attachment of the workman to his tools but had no effect on function, basic design or technique of use. The Nordiska Museet in Stockholm displays a fine collection of carved planes, which were especially widespread in Scandinavia, including several which were owned by a mid-eighteenth century king of Sweden, Adolf Fredrik. Such is the attraction of woodworking that history indicates Adolf Fredrik showed more interest in joining pieces of wood together than in joining the Swedish political parties of the period to his policy. As a result his kingly authority suffered substantially.

The bullnose plane, a rather rare type, may also be included among the smoothing planes. Usually rather small, this plane differed from other wooden stock planes in that the blade is mounted on the front of the stock and is secured to the stock with a wood screw which goes through a slot in the blade. It can be used to plane a surface which is broken by a perpendicular shoulder, or to smooth the insides of a finished drawer where a regular smoothing plane cannot be used because the sides, front or back limit the movement of the tool.

While generally used for smoothing only, smoothing planes may also be used to create hip panels. Those used to champfer cross grain should be equipped with a skew blade.

Radius planes and compass planes are used to smooth the inside or outside of arcs cut in wood, such items as the curved lintels of doors and windows in houses or cabinets. Older radius and compass planes with wooden stocks were required in several sizes to fit different sized work. In the late nineteenth century a combination radius-compass plane was devised which has a flexible sole attached to a cast iron stock. With easy adjustments this combination type may be used for smoothing the inside or outside of any size arc. A few cabinetmakers and carriagemakers used molding planes with stocks which curved on the long axis of the sole. These were to form arched pieces of molding to be attached to pieces of furniture and carriages.

Molding planes, the most glamorous and varied of all the types of modern stocked planes, are different from the smoothing planes only in the thickness of the stock and the shape of sole and blade. They are used and maintained with exactly the same basic techniques.

The most common molding planes are known as ploughs and rounds, both terms being descriptive of function. Ploughs have a convex sole with the edge of the blade ground to match the shape of the sole and, as might be guessed, are used to plough a concave shape in a board. The round, also known as a forkstaff, performs an opposite function. Its concave sole, with blade, or bit, ground to fit, carves a convex surface in wood. The soles of most rounds consisted of about a 90° to 100°

Plane with horn

Bullnose plane in use

Sections of plough and round

Combining ploughs and round
to produce moldings

arc, but some with a full 180° arc may be used for shaping bannisters.

Ploughs and rounds in the old days were usually bought in sets of matching pairs. The numbers of planes in each set consisted of from usually nine to fifteen. Many eighteenth century planters in Virginia, however, including George Washington, ordered up to fifty planes at a time from factories in England.

Pre-industrial age woodworkers could produce an infinite number of molding designs by using a combination of ploughs and rounds in various sizes.

Ploughs can be used alone to cut fluting in columns or parts of furniture, and rounds may be used, sometimes in combination with the rabbeting planes, to create the common but beautiful thumbnail molding so often found on the edges of desk and table tops.

The most common form of special molding plane is the cove, shaped something like a round with shoulders, or stop surfaces, on each side of the convexity. Another common design is the door molding plane with a convoluted sole suitable for shaping a door mold, a stop surface being incorporated into the sole. Ogee planes, too, are fairly common in various sizes, al-

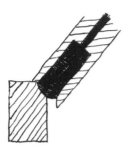

Position of cove plane in use

Section of door molding plane

Section of ogee molding plane

though using a cove and a forkstaff in combination produces a most acceptable ogee form. Two unusual planes which may properly be classified as molding planes are the champfer plane and the witchet.

Champfer planes consist of a solid block of square section with a 90° V-groove cut in the sole. The blade, wedged in, has a straight edge which protrudes through the sole at any desired depth, the edge forming the base of a triangle. When the edge is applied to the corner of a squared timber the corner is champfered and continued planing reduces the corner until the sides of the angled sole stop further cutting. Champfering with such a tool guarantees an exact uniformity not possible with drawknife, spokeshave or smoothing plane.

Witchets are not exactly planes, but they function like planes and are equipped with plane blades secured by wedges. This rather rare tool consists of two blocks each with a 90°

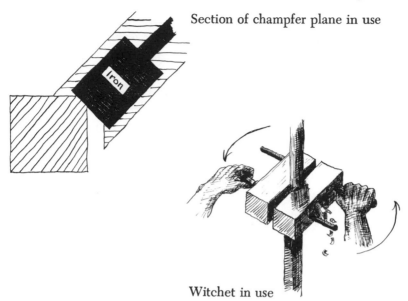

Section of champfer plane in use

Witchet in use

angle cut on the inside surface, held together with two wooden screws, which also allow the distance between the blocks to be adjusted as desired. The witchet may be used to transform a square board into a dowel or to form a round tenon on the end of a square board. The distance between its two blocks is first adjusted to fit the square board being worked then the witchet is rotated so that its blade, which protrudes into the side of the V out in one block, can shave away the corners.

Carriagemakers and some cabinetmakers used numbers of molding planes of many sizes, distinguished from the carpenter's molding planes only by the shape of the stock. For some reason, perhaps because he usually made his own, the carriagemaker's planes frequently have a graceful horn on the front of the stock and many had very short soles or soles cut to a convex or concave shape on the long axis so that they can be used as compass or radius planes, a feature not found in regular molding planes. Undoubtedly the carriagemaker's planes are the most beautiful of woodworking tools, almost all of them exhibiting extremely fine workmanship and graceful shape. Many of them are no longer than two inches, exquisite small jewels capable of exquisite work.

Muntin planes, for forming the muntins in windows, also were available in earlier days as combination planes with one blade to rabbet the wood for the window light and the other to form the molding on the inside of the muntin.

Ordinary rabbetting planes are generally shaped like molding planes but with a flat sole. They are distinguished from smoothing planes by the protrusion of their blades through the sides of the stock as well as the bottom so the blade can cut a corner. Many are equipped with a skew blade for planing cross grain. Most have a sole 2″–2½″ wide.

Special rabbetting planes for small rabbets are usually found with a stop formed in the sole to prevent the blade from cutting too deeply. Some, usually of later vintage, also have a separate fork blade, similar in appearance to the two scribers in a twist bit, wedged into the stock a couple of inches in front of a skew blade. The purpose of the fork is to outline, or scribe, the sides of a rabbet which is cleared by the blade, often a skew blade which is effective on cross grain. Many have a short brass

Carriagemaker's plane

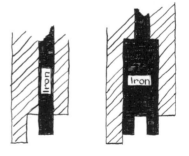

Sections of tongue and groove planes

Combination tongue and groove plane

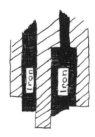

Diagram section of combinati
muntin plane

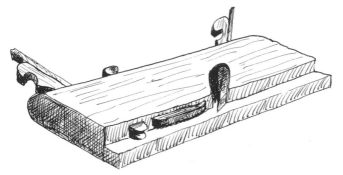

Rabbetting plane with fence, depth gauge and fork

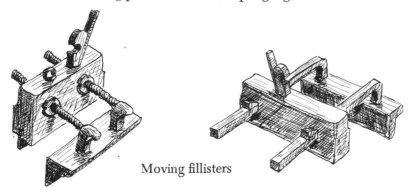

Moving fillisters

sole inlet into the stop surface, adjusted by a brass thumbscrew as a means of controlling the depth of the cut.

The most complex of all old type planes are the moving fillisters, the only function of which is rabbetting. These consist of a heavy stock with a flat sole and, on some, an adjustable depth gauge inset in the sole. Attached to the stock is an adjustable fence attached to two square rods, on older types, which penetrate the stock and are fixed in position by wedges. Later types substitute for the rods two wooden screws with double wooden nuts which fix the distance of fence and stock. Most of the later types of moving fillisters come equipped with eight blades of different widths, starting with a quarter inch and going to three quarters of an inch. These planes can be used to carve rabbets of varying widths and depths at any point on a board up to twelve inches wide. They are most satisfying to use.

Possibly the most common of the rabbetting planes are the

tongue and groove planes which were usually produced in sets of two, one to plough the groove, the other to shape a matching tongue. Sets of tongue and groove planes have wedged blades, as with any other wooden stocked plane, but most are equipped with integral totes, not found on other molding planes. A fairly common occurrence is the combination tongue and groove, one stock with two blades which can separately perform the functions of cutting tongue and groove. Some of these combinations have the blades and wedges raked in the same directions. All have an integral fence to guide the course of the cuts and keep them parallel to the edge of the board being ploughed.

While the largest of the hand planes has blades which seldom exceed two inches in width, about the limit for removing a shaving with the strength of the average workman, there are found a few planes, such as those used for cutting crown mold, with blades three or four inches in width. These usually required either two men or the mechanical help of a winch to to make a smooth cut.

From about 1880 until World War II several American toolmakers offered what is known as a combination plane. This tool, with a cast iron stock and tote and a metal adjustable fence, was sold in a kit which contained as many as thirty different blades, each of which fit into the stock. It can be used to rabbet, to cut tongues and grooves, and to produce molding in many different patterns. Although expensive, it was in great demand by pre-World War II carpenters who worked on jobs away from the shop because it provided the advantages of thirty different planes in one compact package. Combination planes may still be bought in Europe and are available from a few woodworking supply houses in the United States.

All hand planes require virtually the same basic techniques for using, with minor variations in grasp or position in some molding and rabbetting planes. Small one-hand molding planes, of course, are exceptions merely because of size and their use by one hand.

Wooden stocked planes, with the exception of the bullnose, have blades, or irons, secured in position with wooden wedges, straight wedges on smoothing planes and a sort of hooked wedge on molding and rabbetting planes. When blades must be removed for depth adjustment or sharpening, the wedge is removed by tapping the plane with a wooden mallet until the vibrations of the stock loosen the wedge and it and the blade may be removed.

Most smoothing planes that were made during the nineteenth century in England and America have a small knob mortised into the stock in front of the throat, its end grain showing. This is the tapping knob, its only purpose being to provide a point where the stock may be tapped without scarring the stock to loosen the wedge. Tapping should be rapid and firm and never with a metal hammer which will demolish even the tough end grain of the knob.

Other planes without knobs should be tapped on the back end of the stock; again, only with a wooden mallet. Almost all molding and rabbetting planes have wedges with rounded hooks on the apex, the hook, being offset on the forward side of the wedge. These hooks are somewhat beguiling to the beginner; they seem to ask to be tapped on the under side by the

Two types of wedges

mallet, but the beginner who values his tools should resist. Tapping on the hook will indeed loosen and remove the wedge, but after a period of time the hook will split off requiring replacement, a somewhat arduous task which interferes with more productive work. Tap only on the end grain, back or front and maintain the original form of the tool.

All wooden tools are subject to the effects of humidity which cause swelling. When wooden plane stocks and wooden wedges become affected by moisture the two bind together as if glued in position and refuse to loosen under the most adamant tapping. The same problem is incurred with wooden screws and nuts of moving fillisters. When this happens one must place the tool in a warm, dry place close (but certainly not too close) to a source of heat which will, in a short time, dry and shrink the wood and eliminate the binding. The problem may be avoided thereafter by rubbing the wedge or screw with a candle stub, or giving it a light coating of boiled linseed oil. Thereafter either screw or wedge will respond to light tapping or twisting.

One uses exactly the same procedure in sharpening plane irons (or bits, or blades) as in sharpening chisels and gouges. Stone and hone are used exclusively, with stropping on the hand to give a final perfection. Grinding should be resorted to only when careless stoning, which happens occasionally with the most careful of craftsmen, creates a skew or rounded edge on a smoothing plane iron, right for the jack plane but for no others. Of course, the blades of rounds must be sharpened with rounded stones and the edges of blades which cut rather complicated molding may well require several different stones of different shapes and sizes. Extreme attention and care should be given to maintaining the shape of molding plane irons so that iron's edge and cross section of the sole match perfectly.

Stropping the concave edges of the irons of rounds and other molding planes should be done on the edge of the thumb and the heel of the hand where the flesh more nearly fits the concavity of the edge. Smoothing plane irons may be stropped on the palm, as with firming chisels.

Replacing the blade after sharpening so that the proper depth can be attained is sometimes a rather time-consuming task, requiring what seems to be countless removals of the

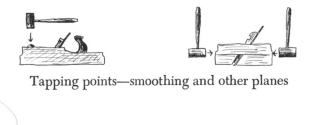

Tapping points—smoothing and other planes

Stropping round plane blade

Replacing smoothing plane blade

wedge and new starts. Sometimes the job must be done over several times, for planes suffer the same diabolical, aberrant characteristics found in all hand tools from time to time. But there are certain techniques which serve to exorcise the demons if one is patient and lucky.

When replacing the iron of a smoothing or rabbetting plane, or a plough, the sole should be placed flat on a board of soft wood laid on the bench top. Rounds and molding planes with concave-edged irons should be held so that the concavity of the sole encloses the corner of the board. The iron is then dropped into its cavity, or, if the fit is tight, pushed in gently until stopped by the board, the edge then being exactly even with the sole. Then the wedge is inserted, pushed tightly in place and tapped smartly with the mallet on its upper end, driving it in slightly to secure the blade. Usually the tapping of the wedge will drive the iron in far enough so that its edge will protrude slightly below the sole, the board on which the plane is set preventing it from protruding too far. A trial on the corner of a piece of scrap will determine whether or not the depth of the blade is correct. If it is not deep enough the top end of the iron may be tapped once with a metal hammer and the plane tried again, this being repeated until the desired depth is attained. If, however, the depth is too deep because the wedge was not tight enough, then the wedge must be removed and the whole procedure gone through once more.

Planing is done most easily when the edge of the iron is set quite shallowly to remove a very thin shaving. At times, however, especially for rough forming, the iron may be set rather deeply so that each stroke removes a relatively thick shaving, thereby saving a great deal of time. One must be careful, however, that the throat of the plane, the space between the edge of the blade and the continuation of the sole beyond the blade cavity, will accommodate the shaving being removed. If the blade is too deep, the throat will quickly be filled with jambed shavings which prevent the plane from cutting. Jack planes normally have a rather wide throat which will take care of rather thick shavings, while trying and joining and molding planes have a narrow throat. The ultimate depth of the iron is utterly dependent on the size of the throat or the worker will create misery for himself and poor work.

After the blade is set it should be sighted along the sole to make sure that the edge is parallel to the surface of the sole. If it is not, the position of the edge may be corrected by tapping the shank of the iron on one side or another with a metal hammer.

It is not unheard of to find old joining and trying planes with soles which have been disfigured from long or unskillful use. There may be long, deep scratches in the sole or it may simply be bowed in the center from wear, making it useless for guiding the blade to cut a level plane. Such inadequacy can easily be corrected by removing wedge and blade and dressing the sole with a smoothing plane, checking the surface continually with a straight edge.

Dressing is accomplished by clamping the stock upside down in the front vise and planing the ends of the sole down to match the level of its center portion. The iron of the smoothing plane should be set very shallowly for this operation. The straight edge should be applied to the dressed sole in every direction, lengthwise, crosswise and diagonally after every two or three strokes. After dressing, the sole should be sighted along its length to check for any inadvertent twist of its plane. Once satisfied that the sole is properly restored the worker should bring it to a state of glassy smoothness by scraping with a metal scraper.

As stated earlier, virtually the same technique is used for all types of planing. It is not a difficult technique to learn or use, but some experience will perfect it to the point it becomes second nature and deeply satisfying. The plane must be pushed evenly down the surface of wood being planed with the right arm and maintained in position with the left.

On jack planes, trying planes and joining planes which have totes, or handles, the right hand grasps the tote with the forearm approximately parallel to the bench top. The strength of upper arm and shoulder, with auxiliary strength coming from the back and legs, then pushes the plane forward. The left hand which grasps the front upper corner of the stock, or the horn on horned planes, presses down slightly and also keeps the stock pointed along the axis of the board.

For long cuts the left hand presses the plane downward at

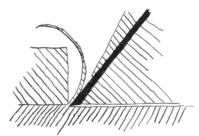

Relation of plane iron depth and size of throat

Sighting blade with sole

the front at the beginning of the cut, and more downward pressure is placed by the right hand at the end of the cut.

The plane is a slicing tool and not a chisel, therefore it functions best in long, continuous cuts of even speed. This is not difficult to follow on long or short boards. For boards of between one and two feet in length the worker may make his cuts without changing his position, only differing the downward pressure by both hands as explained. On boards of from two to five feet he may have to make one step to propel the plane from end to end, again maintaining the downward pressure of back or front of the stock as needed. But on long boards, from six to twelve or fifteen feet in length, he must take several steps along the length of the board, keeping an even downward pressure on back and front between the first six inches of the cut and the last. The evenness of his pressure, and the test of his skill and acquired intuition, can be determined by the length of the shavings which curl from the throat of the plane like tendrils of maiden's hair to cover the floor and bench top with a fragrant and crinkly carpet. The shavings should be as long as the strip being planed.

Children can add to the satisfaction of the planer working on long boards. The fresh coiled shavings, long and springy, offer admirable material for wigs and mustaches and curly beards, the wearer's imagination offering vicarious pleasure to the adult intent upon his work.

There are boards, especially the long ones, which in their length will have a spot of peculiar grain which does not shave smoothly but breaks through the planed surface to create problems of splinters and roughness and bruises, especially on soft woods. These problems may be solved in several ways: The peculiar grain may be planed from both directions until smooth; a skew-bladed plane may be used on that portion of the surface; or the plane may be held so that the edge of the iron is askew to the axis of the board while the movement of the plane follows the axis.

One must be especially careful when planing the edges of boards to keep the plane even athwart. The surface should be checked from both ends after every couple of strokes and corrected if need be with the next stroke.

One of the problems in smoothing long or short boards is that the surface at the beginning of the stroke tends to end higher than that in the middle, and the surface at the end of the stroke tends to be lower. The problem is one of varying pressure during the entire shot and can be corrected with experience and attention to certain principles which apply to planes.

One must remember that the surface of the sole before the edge of the iron guides the plane before the cut, and the sole behind the iron guides it after the cut. In starting the cut, then, the plane is placed so that the front of the sole rests solidly on the board with the blade edge about a half inch from the end. The plane is then pushed forward while steady downward pressure holds the forward part of the sole solidly on the board, forcing the cut to be level and true. At the end of the cut more pressure is put on the rear of the stock, which supports the plane and guides the cut after the front part of the sole extends beyond the farther end of the board. If not enough pressure is put on the front at the beginning of the cut, the cut has a bad beginning. If the pressure is relieved on the rear of the plane at the end of the cut the front tends to dip, creating an uneven cut.

Despite the generally greater efficiency and effectiveness of the long stroke, some jobs of planing require short, savage strokes. Jack planing, for instance, is often done with a short stroke which explains the series of cupped surfaces found on some old jack-planed boards instead of the long shallow troughs found on others. Also the smoothing plane is sometimes used with short strokes when dressing down the minute irregularities left from planing with trying or joining plane. Indeed, short strokes are more effective when forming hip panels across grain with the smoothing plane. For this job, however, it helps to have two smoothing planes, one with the blade set to maximum effective depth to do the rough cutting, another with the blade at minimum effective depth to smooth.

In forming hip panels with the smoothing plane no guide is necessary if the champfered portion is to be inside the paneling where it will not be seen. But where the hip molding is in view a thin straight board should be tacked or clamped to the surface of the panel at the highest intended point of the

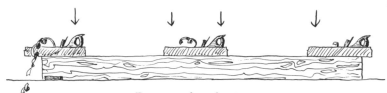

Pressure for planing

Holding plane askew

Section showing guide board
on hip panel

Angled cut for crossgrain planing

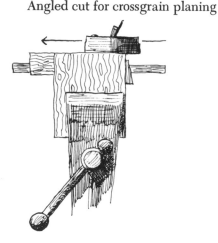

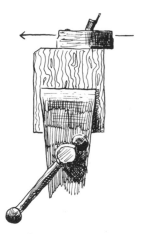

Scrap stop for crossgrain planing

molding to keep its corner straight. The side of the smoothing
plane is guided by this board when the molding is cut deeply
enough to start forming its upper corner. Such a guide is also
needed when a large arched plough plane is used to form concave hip panels.

One thing to watch in using the smoothing plane to make
hip panels, or in edge planing where a cross-grained surface
must be worked, is the order in which cross grain and straight
grain are planed. Cross grain should always be planed first so
that any portion of the grain which breaks off at the end of the
stroke may be corrected with subsequent straight-grain planing.
There are two methods, however, by which the bruising at the
end of a cross-grain stroke may be avoided.

The simplest method is to saw off the corner at the end of the cross-grained surface at a 45° angle. This method, however, may only apply when the adjacent straight-grained edge will later be reduced enough to eliminate the angled cut. The other method is to clamp a scrap of board tightly adjacent to the end of the cross grain, the grain of the scrap being perpendicular to the grain of the board being planed. This scrap supports the end of the cross grain and keeps it from bruising. Of course, the plane passes over the entire length of the scrap as though it were a continuation of the cross grain. The second method may be used for smoothing, molding and rabbetting of cross-grained surfaces.

Molding planes require the same techniques in use as smoothing planes, the only difference being that the molding planes, with the exception of the tongue and groove, have no tote. Accordingly, the rounded rear upper corner is nestled snugly in the palm of the right hand, the fingers extending over the side of the stock to secure the grasp. The left hand is placed in the same position as with smoothing planes, except with horned molding planes used by the carriagemaker. On the horned planes the left thumb is hooked over the horn to assist the right hand in propelling the plane.

Only the grasp of the right hand differs in the technique of using the moving fillister. Here the cross rod or screw stock is held by the right hand, pulling the fence, which is to the right, tightly against the side of the stuff being planed.

Cove molding planes, and a few others, are not held vertically but at a slight angle to the left. The proper angle is determined by the stop surface on the right of the sole. This surface is placed so that it glides solidly on the upper surface of the stuff, which places the stock at its proper angle for planing.

The presence of stops on certain molding and rabbetting planes automatically eliminates the problem of an uneven surface as is faced when using the trying and joining planes. With a stopped plane the motion is continued until the blade no longer produces a shaving anywhere on the surface being formed. When shavings cease to be produced one last stroke should be made with extra downward pressure, which sometimes yields a few wisps of wood from minute vestigial heights.

Many of the molding and rabbetting planes have integral fences which serve to guide the stroke in line relative to the edge of the board. Those lacking fences, however, may have them temporarily appended, a practice followed by most old-time woodworkers, as is evidenced by tack or screw holes seen on the sides of many old rabbetting and molding planes. All that is needed is a thin board about two inches wide and as long as the stock of the plane. This is screwed or tacked or clamped with a C-clamp to the side of the stock so that its lower edge extends perhaps a half inch lower than the sole. Such temporary fences serve as well as built-in ones to control the path of the plane. Depending on need, several narrower boards may be placed between the stock and the fence to adjust the distance of the fence from the stock. On wide-soled rabbetting planes this fence may consist of a narrow thin board attached to the sole itself when a cut the whole width of the blade is not required.

Holding the moving fillister

Plane with fence and stop appended

Adjustable sole fence

Temporary stops are also easily appended to rabbetting and some molding planes. They consist only of a narrow board attached to the side of the stock with the edge of the board at a proper distance above the sole to match the depth of the intended cut.

Small one-handed planes follow the same principles as larger planes but the technique of use necessarily is different because only one hand is involved. The small planes are held by the tips of the fingers and thumb, as with holding a block of wood one picks up from the floor. Usually, as the short sole indicates, they are used on short pieces of molding with strokes the length of the work. The technique of their use closely resembles the use of a brush, mainly done with wrist motion, care being taken to hold the sole solidly on the surface being planed.

Several adjuncts to the plane make the job of finishing, molding and joining easier and more accurate. These include the shooting board, usually referred to as a molding board by cabinetmakers, the miter block and various scrapers.

The shooting board consists of two boards at least six feet long, both of them straight and true and preferably quarter sawn (with the grain running perpendicular to the width) one of them eight to ten inches wide, the other four to five inches wide. These boards are screwed, pegged or glued together, the narrower one on top of the wider with one edge of each coincidental with one edge of the other. More careful woodworkers might wish to place small boards a quarter inch thick and an inch wide every four or five inches crossways between the two

Shooting board in use

before fastening, to allow air circulation which will prevent subsequent warping. The top board is pierced with holes to receive bench stops or is rabbetted across its width close to one end to receive a block of wood which serves as a stop.

In use the board to be planed is placed on the narrow top surface of the shooting board, its end tightly against the stop, its inside edge protruding perhaps a sixteenth of an inch beyond the inner edge of the top board. The joining or trying plane is then placed on its side on the lower board and pushed the length of the board to pare, accurately and mechanically, its edge smooth and square. Action is stopped by the inner surface of the upper board, which also serves to guide the plane. Sometimes a strip of paper is glued to the inner edge of the upper board which, when shaved by the plane bit, indicates when planing should cease.

Another stop device applicable only to shooting, as such planing is called, consists of a thin board of the same width as the thickness of the upper portion of the shooting board. This is screwed or tacked onto the underlying wood of the sole of the plane on its left edge, covering part of the edge of the iron. When this strip touches the edge of the upper portion of the shooting board the cutting of the plane is stopped. Of course, the edge of the board being planed must extend a greater distance to compensate for the thickness of the strip on the plane's sole.

Whenever a board must have a mitered edge a special shooting board must be used. The mitered shooting board is very much like the regular variety, but has the upper board slanted at precisely a 45° angle so that the edge of any board resting there will be planed to an exact 45°.

The mitered corners of molding for picture frames and decorations may be trued with a device called a miter block, similar in functional priniciple to the shooting board. In effect the miter block is a small portable vise with both jaws, one of which is movable, cut on one side to a precise 45° angle. A piece of molding previously cut in the miter box is clamped between the jaws by means of a wooden screw, the cut end of the molding protruding perhaps a sixteenth of an inch beyond the angled surface of the blocks. Then a something plane is used to dress the saw cut on the molding. As with the shooting board,

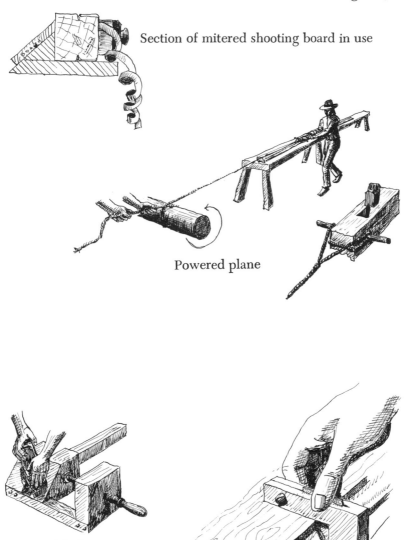

Section of mitered shooting board in use

Powered plane

Miter block in use

Molding scraper in use

paper is pasted onto the angled faces of the blocks to act as a telltale when the plane has cut deeply enough.

Planes with blades three or more inches wide, such as those used to shape crown mold, usually used a source of power other than the planer. These large planes often had a short rod inserted across the forestock to which a rope was attached. An apprentice could then provide additional power to pull the plane, or he could wrap the rope around a winch to provide power. The planer only guided the plane.

Scraping was used more than sanding to give a finished surface to furniture in the eighteenth and early nineteenth centuries, and specially shaped scrapers were used to finish the surface of molding. Molding scrapers are no more than a small block of wood cut with an offset across the width and split with a saw through the edge almost to the end. Into this split at the corner of the offset a piece of sheet steel previously cut to fit the shape of the moldings is inserted and secured with a wood screw or a clinched nail. The wide part of the offset acts as a fence, the narrow part, which is held uppermost, as a stop. When drawn down the length of a piece of molding the steel blade scrapes it to satiny smoothness.

The stocks of wooden planes should be kept coated with wax or boiled linseed oil to minimize swelling and drying and subsequent checking. Irons should be kept lightly oiled and sharpening stones should be kept readily at hand. Properly maintained and used, an adequate variety of planes is a thing of beauty to hold and behold and a rare pleasure to use.

CHAPTER X

Turning

LATHES are the oldest of man's woodworking machines. So simple are they, and so adaptable to new conditions, they have been readily converted with no change in principle to machining metal and to operating by the new sources of power which have appeared since the Romans pioneered in producing waterpower before the Christian era. Also lathes, in one type or another, are so easy to make that they are found in frontier farm workshops as well as in sophisticated cabinet shops.

A lathe is no more than a source of power which continuously turns a stick between two fixed points so that a cutting tool held against the stick will shape it to some desired design. The only major differences in the first prehistoric lathe and those used in professional woodworking shops of the 1970s is the source of power, outside the worker, and constant rotation of the piece of work being turned. No principles have been altered in all that time.

The earliest form of lathe, still being used in many parts of the world including the United States is no more than two logs, or heavy beams stuck in the ground with a pointed pin in one and a pointed screw at the same level in the other. Stuff being turned is fixed in its longitudinal center between these points and held there by the tightening of the screw. Before the use of screws, one of the points was probably held in place by a small wedge after being driven into the center of the stuff.

Power to turn the stuff comes from a long primitive treadle and springy pole, or lath, attached to the ceiling joists above the lathe or, for outdoor installations, from a springy, growing limb of a tree, with a strap stretched between the two. The strap wraps once around the stuff and is held taut by the spring of the lath. When the treadle is depressed the strap rotates the stuff rapidly; when the treadle is released the spring of the lath rotates the stuff in the opposite direction, returning it to its original position, a matter of simplicity itself. Shaping is done by holding a turning chisel against the stuff on the downward

Pole lathe

Bow lathe

Great wheel lathe in use

stroke of the treadle, removing it on the reciprocal motion, and repeating the process until the stuff is formed. During turning, the chisel rests on a small board fastened between the two parts, its top edge slightly above the center axis of the stuff.

This simple device, with its somewhat wasteful reciprocating motion, has been used over the millennia to produce some extraordinarily delicate turnings for chair parts and backs, bed posts and tool handles. Professional cabinetmakers used it until the seventeenth century.

Another form of the reciprocating lathe, found in the Middle East and the Orient, is powered by a bow with its string wrapped once around the stuff like the string of a bow drill around the chuck. A disadvantage of the bow lathe is that it either requires another man to operate or requires the turner to power the lathe with one hand while he holds his turning chisel with the other.

Most English and American cabinet shops of the eighteenth century discarded the pole lathe for the greater efficiency of the great wheel lathe which turns the stuff continually in one direction, allowing it to operate full time rather than only half time. Its name comes from a wheel some six feet in diameter mounted separately about eight feet from the headstock of the lathe. The lathe itself has a six to twelve foot bed of heavy timbers with a headstock consisting of a free turning spindle with a pulley and a prong, or fork, which extends through the front block of the head stock and holds one end of the work. Since the prong transmits the motion of the pulley to the work it has a sharp point in its exact center flanked by two shallow chisel edges which are forced into the end of the work

The tail stock, which rides on the two stout rails of the lathe bed, is a heavy wooden block which slides and can be secured by wedge or bolt at any desired distance from the head stock. A screw with a conical point on one end and a crank on the other pierces the tail block exactly in line with the prong of the head stock. This screw holds the other end of the work tightly. A sliding rest for supporting turning chisels is attached to the bed between head stock and tail stock. Power to operate this type lathe is supplied by an apprentice who turns the great wheel steadily at a speed directed by the turner.

Foot lathe

Early in the nineteenth century the great wheel lathe was superseded by the foot lathe, its only basic difference from the great wheel type being that the pulley is operated by a belt around a flywheel mounted directly beneath the pulley and activated by a treadle. The foot lathe can be operated by the turner himself, eliminating the need for an apprentice with a sense of rhythm and great stamina. In all other respects the foot lathe is exactly like the great wheel lathe.

Frequently in the old days, when a shop was located near a stream, the lathe was powered by a waterwheel, allowing the turner to concentrate on his work.

All types of lathes can be designed or adapted to different kinds of turning. For instance, the pole lathes used by British bowl turners up until recently, had no tail stock and substituted a face plate for the prong. A block of wood can be screwed to the face plate and worked on its end grain. Face plates can also be installed on regular lathes, usually being screwed on a threaded prong, for turning lamp standards, circular decorations and other flat turned pieces.

When turning large pieces on the great wheel or foot lathes the prong and its chisel edges have a tendency to spread the end grain of the work, becoming loose and throwing the work off center while being turned. This problem was solved early in the nineteenth century by using a hollow spindle which projects in front of the head stock. An immovable fork with a point but no chisel edges is inserted through the spindle. In front of the stock on the spindle there is a pulley which has a metal elbow extending over the work and rotating around it. A metal collar with a projection, called a driver, which engages the elbow and is turned by its action, is clamped around the work itself. Held between two immovable pointed spindles the work turns truly without being damaged by the opposite pressures of turning tools and chisel edges on the prong.

By the end of the eighteenth century the ingenious French had perfected a lathe which would turn gunstocks, furnishing a concept for the production template lathes used to make thousands of duplicate turnings in late twentieth century woodworking factories.

Seventeenth-, eighteenth- and early nineteenth-century turners usually constructed their own lathes, each showing only minor differences from all others; for instance, the difference of wooden and wrought-iron head stocks and bearings. Since about 1870, however, lathes with cast iron beds and pulleys have been furnished by industrial toolmakers. The ancient unchangeable form has been easily adapted to steam and electric power.

There is as much variety in the designs of the chisels used to carve turning wood as there is in molding planes. One finds chisels for infinite functions, some flat, some with curved edges

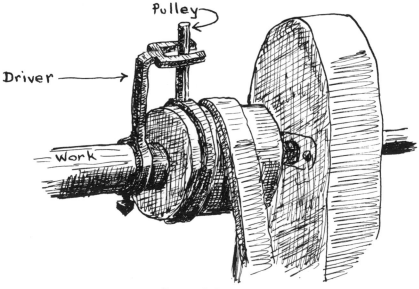

Pulley and driver

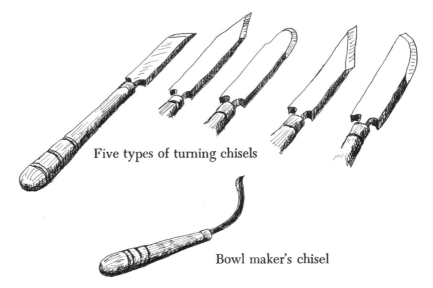

Five types of turning chisels

Bowl maker's chisel

and, in addition, pointers and skew points and beads, for the chisels of the turner perform the same basic function as the molding planes but on a different dimension. All have flat blades and those with curved edges perform the work of gouges.

The blades of turning chisels are usually rather short, not more than six inches long, with handles from nine inches to a foot in length so that they may be grasped with both hands. Turning chisels which show little difference from those used in the seventeenth century are still available today from a number of manufacturers.

The ancient turner, however, had the advantage of being able to seek out a blacksmith to make his chisels of his own design and temper them according to his own tastes. And, of course, the old-time turner almost invariably turned his own handles to fit his taste and the size of his hands, providing him better control over his creations.

In Wales and parts of England, Scotland and Ireland, bowlmakers required special chisels not suitable for anything but making bowls. Bowls of the type made in rural Britain were produced, and are still produced in one or two places, on a foot- or water-powered lathe equipped with a face plate. The stuff is a section of log, up to a foot in diameter and six inches long, which is expected to yield as many as half a dozen bowls of

different sizes. Special thin chisels with curved shanks are necessary for such work, and the bowlmaker uses one chisel for
each of the bowls, turning them out one by one, starting with
a small bowl in the center and continuing until the largest possible is formed on its inside. The largest is finished on the outside with a conventional turning chisel.

Also, since chair posts and legs and back spindles, bed posts
and drawer handles and decorations must duplicate an original, the turner used a number of calipers to measure precisely
the outside and inside dimensions as well as distances between
moldings. Wheelwrights, who turned wagon wheel hubs, usually on water-powered lathes, had a most graceful design for
double calipers which set the outside measurements of two
dimensions found on the hubs they turned and kept the set
until four identical hubs had been produced.

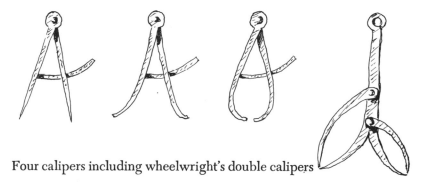

Four calipers including wheelwright's double calipers

Rhythm is the secret of even, tireless turning on the pole
lathe, the great wheel lathe and the foot lathe, a rhythm which
beats with the heart and adjusts itself to the size of stuff being
worked and the type of wood. Soft coarse-grained wood, particularly of large dimensions should be turned at a slower speed than
hard, close-grained stuff, and the turner must adjust the speed
of his rhythm to his work.

An additional rhythm, of the hands and arms, is required
for the pole lathe because of its reciprocating action. Shaping
on the lathe is a result of cutting with the chisel, not scraping.
This can only be done on a pole lathe with the downstroke of the
treadle. When the spring pole returns to its original position,

rotating the stuff away from the turner, the chisel must be lifted slightly to clear the stuff and save the chisel edge. As the treadle is once more depressed the chisel is again placed in its cutting position.

The tool rest, often no more than a long strip of wood fastened to the headstock and tailstock of a pole lathe, should be at a height that will allow the chisel edge to be slightly above the center axis of the stuff when its bottom surface is placed on the rest.

For soft woods the angle between a tangent on the stuff at the point the chisel edge touches it and the line of the basil should be about 30°. For hard woods this angle should be about 40° to 45°, requiring that the rest be lowered slightly. The relative position of the center axis of the wood and the position of the chisels also applies to end turning as in making bowls.

Although a square stick can have its corners cut off on the lathe, the old turners usually resorted to reducing all corners of a piece of wood to be turned before placing it on the lathe.

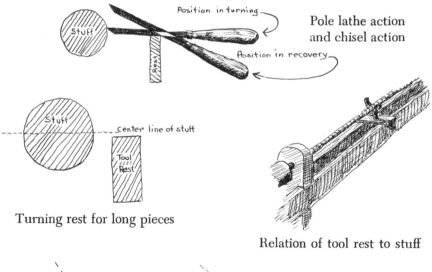

Pole lathe action and chisel action

Turning rest for long pieces

Relation of tool rest to stuff

Angles of chisel to stuff for soft and hard woods

Much effort can be saved by using the drawknife or hatchet to round off the corners before turning.

Special turning rests are used when shaping long, delicate pieces which might sag in the center or chatter against the chisel if not supported. Such rests may be made of wood or metal. They should be designed to brace the work on its side directly opposite the turner as well as support it on its bottom side.

Some specialty turners, mostly of the nineteenth century, employed a number of special devices for their work. There is a hollow tube made to fit on the prong in which a hollow cylinder of wood can be fixed and turned on its inside for special purposes such as patternmaking. There are also special face plates, some with a screw in the center large enough to hold a flat piece of wood securely while it is being turned. Other face plates, made to turn work in which a screw hold in the bottom will be unsightly, are designed for the work to be temporarily glued to the plate with four small spikes around its edge to provide purchase against the pressure of the chisel. Still others are pierced with a number of holes through which wood screws are inserted and screwed into the stuff.

It should be pointed out, in connection with all old woodworking techniques, that the craftsmen of past centuries, the master craftsmen certainly, displayed a singular ingenuity, in solving the problems of production by hand work. The old craftsmen were no less interested in labor saving than their descendants of the Electronic Age. But while each tiny improvement in tool or technique led the race of man inexorably toward the Industrial Age which destroyed handcraftsmanship, the old craftsman must be given great credit for not deserting

Three types of face plates

the standards of good taste and fine art merely to save his energy. If such attitudes can be revived, the rebirth of interest in fine handcraftsmanship will add immeasurable values to our modern industrial society.

So, if the culturally reincarnate turner of the late twentieth century, using a pole lathe or foot lathe or great wheel lathe, perhaps made by himself, has original ideas that will make his work easier or better he should not put them aside. He should use them, confident that his attitude is as authentic as his tools.

Lathes should be maintained as carefully as other tools. Moving parts should be kept lubricated to minimize wear and maintain accuracy. Wooden parts should be protected from the ravages of moisture and insects. The metal parts, including the blades of turning chisels, should be coated lightly with oil to keep them clean and rust free.

Above all, turning chisels must be kept sharpened, for a sharp tool is the most efficient labor-saving device enjoyed by the handcraftsman. Turning chisels are shapened exactly as firming and paring chisels and the irons of planes.

Also the turner should have his tools placed in an orderly manner within easy reach while he stands at his lathe. A bench alongside the lathe, a shelf overhead or a tool rack attached to the lathe bed are all satisfactory. Each turner should devise a means of placing his tools most sutiable to his personality and method of work. In hand turning each individual is his own authority on such matters.

CHAPTER XI

Miscellany

BESIDES the major categories of tools and techniques described in previous chapters there are a number of other important woodworking tools used in earlier times which require experience more than technique. The striking tools, hammer and mallet and maul, are certainly basic, but the techniques of using each are quickly described.

As in the 1970s, old carpenters and cabinetmakers used hammers and mallets without giving a great deal of thought to how they are used for maximum efficiency.

Carpenters since ancient times have used the claw hammer for driving and pulling iron nails. Claw hammers are available in different weights for different work, a heavy hammer being useful, for instance, in driving nails into tough wood without bending the nails. Many an amateur can salvage many a nail if he chooses a big hammer for the job instead of a lightweight one which has not the bulk to drive a nail into tough grain wood but is heavy enough to bend the nail itself.

Accuracy in hitting the nail squarely is certainly a factor in nailing and while accuracy is largely based on experience, the manner in which a hammer is grasped is also important. First of all, the handle should be held at its end, not halfway up the handle, in order to take advantage of the full momentum imparted by the length of the handle. Its end should just protrude from the heel of the hand with the fingers wrapped around the handle and the thumb either laid along its axis or wrapped around above the fingers. The long axis of the handle should follow the line of

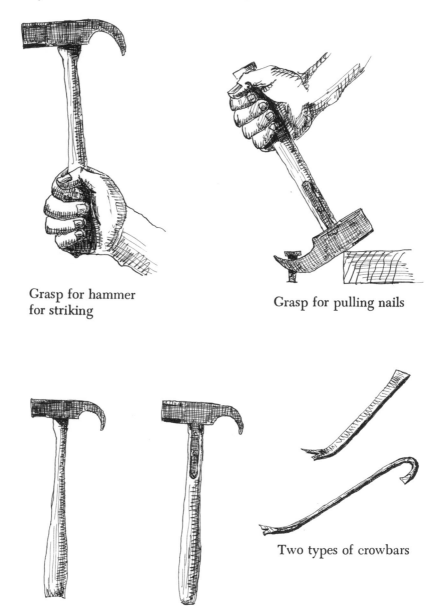

Grasp for hammer
for striking

Grasp for pulling nails

Two types of crowbars

Old type hammers, with and without straps

the wrist and forearm for maximum accuracy, as the hammer is really no more than an extension of the arm.

In pulling nails with the claw the position of the handle should be reversed in the hand with the claw pointing either forward or backward. The closer the hand is to the end of the handle the more leverage may be applied to pulling the nail.

Before the adz eye hammer was invented about 1840 most claw hammers were made of a square or round bar of iron or steel, pierced in the middle to form an eye and with the claws formed on one end. This design, which was common from Roman times until the beginning of the Industrial Age, gave little support to the handle in pulling nails, and it took very little nail pulling to loosen the handle to the point that the tool no longer accurately drove nails. This problem was solved to some extent by welding to the head two iron straps which extended down the handle and were bradded there to give support to the claw. The straps, however, destroyed the springiness of the handle and reduced the efficiency of the hammer as a driving tool.

Until the adz eye hammer made its appearance, most carpenters kept with them a crow, or crowbar, to be used exclusively for pulling nails. The crow is a bar of steel from one to three feet long with one end fashioned into a claw and with a curve formed near the claw to act as a fulcrum when prising nails from wood. Nail-pulling was not a great problem, however, until mass produced cut nails became available in quantity after 1800 and buildings began to be built more and more with nails instead of mortise and tenon joints secured with wooden pegs. This change in the technology of house building led to the design of the adz eye hammer which provided enough support to the handle in the elongated eye to make it an effective nail-pulling tool without altering its efficiency in driving nails. Many carpenters before 1800 used a light cross pein (or peen) hammer for nailing clapboards or molding in place.

Cabinetmakers, who preferred glue to nails, seldom used a claw hammer. Instead they preferred a light cross pein hammer and later adopted the Warrington hammer, either cross pein or straight pein, with its peculiar spread pein. About the only use the cabinetmaker had for a metal hammer was in driving the small nails used to secure decorative molding in place while the glue dried.

And while only indirectly connected with woodworking, the upholsterer used a light tack hammer which, before 1870, was a most graceful tool, with long slim head, a short claw formed on its poll, and with a slim springy handle.

Tack hammers tapped the sharp tacks in the wood rather

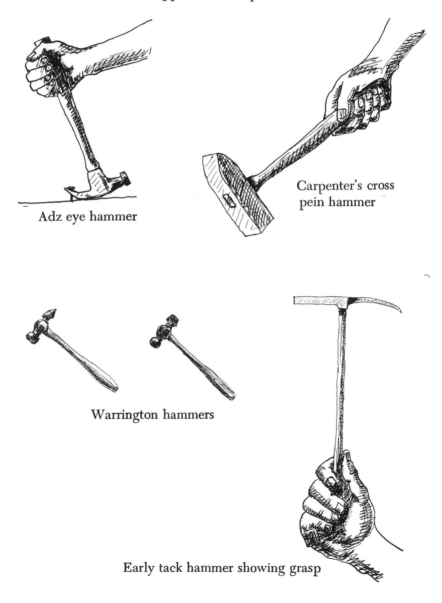

Adz eye hammer

Carpenter's cross pein hammer

Warrington hammers

Early tack hammer showing grasp

than driving them, and a short stroke allowed the spring of the handle to do most of the work. They are held a little differently, with the end of the handle in the center of the palm and with only two fingers and the thumb grasping the handle. Such a grasp allows freer motion of the wrist, which, instead of the arm, does the work in driving tacks.

Handles for hammers are most important both for accuracy and for comfort. Old carpenters, cabinetmakers and upholsterers invariably made their own handles from hickory and swamp ash in America and usually from ash in Europe. They may be shaped with drawknife and spokeshave, or whittled with a pocket knife, before being scraped smooth with steel scraper or a piece of broken glass.

Hammer handles should be made the proper length to provide utmost momentum with each blow without unduly tiring the worker. The portion that is grasped should be the proper dimension to fit the size of the individual worker's hand and offer a firm grip without cramping the fingers. The part immediately below the eye, in all types of hammers, should be strong, certainly in a carpenter's claw hammer, but slim enough to impart some spring, and the extra momentum thereof, to each blow.

Before the era of mass-produced nails, when all nails were made singly by hand in blacksmith shops or nail factories, there was far more variety in the types but less choice in sizes. Hand wrought nails were expensive and used sparingly in building and cabinetwork. Rose-headed nails were the common nails of the preindustrial period, but also available for special uses were T-head nails, L-head nails, tenterhooks, brads, or broad-headed nails, flat-headed spikes, tacks, staples, nails with flattened points for greater holding ability, and others.

T-head and L-head types were used for finishing nails in fastening floor boards to joists and in joining the components of stairs. The axis of the head on this type nail should be in the same direction as the grain of the wood into which it is driven so that the head will not protrude above the surface.

Small flat-headed nails were used to tack molding to furniture and slightly larger ones were used by carpenters to secure door, window and crown mold in houses. To prevent the wedge-shaped nail shank from splitting thin molding, a brad awl should be employed to bore a hole through the molding before the nail is driven.

All hand-wrought nails have a four-sided shank which is drawn to a sharp point. Cut nails, which first appeared in America around 1790, are tapered in one dimension but the other two sides of the shank are parallel. The ends of cut nails are square rather than pointed, and the heads are flat and rectangular in shape. Thin lumber fastened with cut nails is less likely to split because the flat end of the nail tends to punch its way through the wood fibers, creating its own entry and obviating the need for a brad awl.

The old time carpenter had no compunctions about driving nails completely through two boards, as in batten doors, and clinching the point of the nail on the inside of the work to maximize holding power.

Cut nails, in limited sizes and with only vestigial heads, are readily available in the 1970s, but they have been largely replaced by wire nails of infinite sizes and types which are mass produced more quickly and more cheaply. Wire nails were first produced in England in the 1850s and became popular in America mainly because of a lower price, during the 1880s and 1890s, within the period of hand carpentry. They have always been available in two major types, the common nail, with a flat circular head, and the finishing nail, with a rudimentary head which is no more than a slight swelling in the top of the shank.

All nails, hand wrought, cut and wire, should be driven with hard blows for penetration and tapping blows for setting the head. Otherwise, the face of the hammer will drive the nail head below the surface and mar the surface of the board being nailed, an occurrence of which an old-time carpenter would be most ashamed.

Wire finishing nails should be driven in with the hammer until the head projects about a sixteenth of an inch. They should be driven the rest of the way and into the wood by using a nail set, a short steel rod with tapered end and flat point which is placed on the nail head and tapped smartly with the hammer.

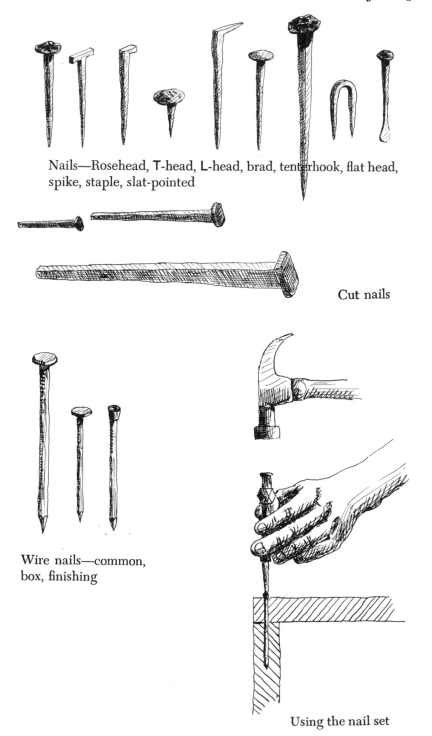

Nails—Rosehead, **T**-head, **L**-head, brad, tenterhook, flat head, spike, staple, slat-pointed

Cut nails

Wire nails—common, box, finishing

Using the nail set

Before the era of mass-produced nails the main fastening device for the frames of houses, mills and bridges was the wood peg, usually designated a trunnel, which is a corruption of the ancient term *treenail*. Most trunnels used before 1840 were cut square then driven into the round peg hole of mortise and tenon with a maul or mallet. Since the timbers of each wall of a mortised building were fitted together on the ground before raising, the housewright or millwright would use a guide pin, a roughly whittled pin with a hooked head, to test the juxtaposition of peg holes before driving the trunnel home.

The use of trunnels practically disappeared after 1840 in house building, but the builders of wooden bridges, particularly covered bridges, used them to pin the timbers together almost until World War I. Bridge makers used mass-produced trunnels, round instead of square, but preferred over spikes and bolts because wood in wood held up longer under the vibration and tension of constant traffic by iron-shod horses and heavy wagons.

Many cabinetmakers strengthened mortise and tenon joints in chairs, beds, chest of drawers and tables with small trunnels, cut square like those of the housewright and driven home with

Trunnel

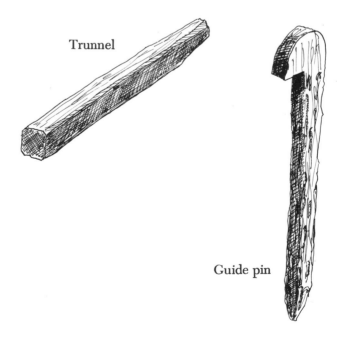

Guide pin

a light mallet, then, using a dowel saw, cut off flush with the outside surface.

For the most part, however, cabinetmakers eschewed nails or trunnels and relied upon carefully fitted mortises and tenons bonded together with animal glue. The glue is made from the sticky residue of boiled cows' horns and hooves. It must be applied with a brush while hot, for otherwise it hardens into a useless mass. Animal glue is dispensed from a heavy cast iron or lead pot which held the heat and the liquidity of the glue. When iron pots are used they are often set on a small iron stand, or spider, so that the cabinetmaker's apprentice can keep the glue hot by periodically burning a small pile of shavings beneath the pot.

Animal glue used to fasten the joints of antique furniture is not effective unless the two pieces being joined are clamped tightly together until the glue is thoroughly dry. Consequently a number of different types of clamps were devised and used by the old-time cabinetmakers. Some of them are of metal but most, in the ancient tradition of woodworkers, were of wood.

Glue pot on spider

Many of these clamps in modified form are still available to modern woodworkers of commercial and avocational status, but the modern types have many metal parts and are mass produced while the types, especially before 1800, were often made in the shop as needed.

Bar clamps are used for clamping two or three boards together for joining on their edges, as in making a table top, or for clamping the rails and legs of a chair together. Several types have been used over the centuries.

One is a three- or four-foot iron bar, either square or round, with a knob upset on one end, this end being bent back parallel to the original bar for about three inches. A flat plate of iron with a turn screw in one end and a hole slightly larger than the bar in the other end is slipped on the bar and set at a slightly longer distance from the knob than the widths of the boards being joined. One tightens the screw to clamp the pieces, the pressure of the screw tilting the plate enough to jamb it against the bar, thereby setting it immovably in position.

Bar clamps of wood were more popular in the old days because they could be made in the shop and were less likely to mar the wood being glued. All were similar in design, consisting of a long strong board perhaps two inches square with an offset

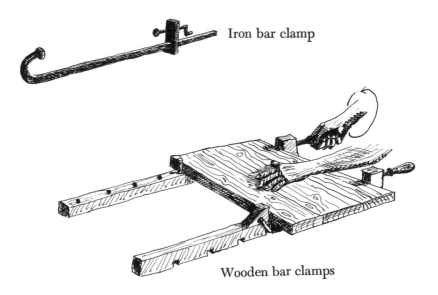

Iron bar clamp

Wooden bar clamps

boss sawed in or pegged to one end, the boss being pierced with a threaded hole to receive a wooden screw. As with the iron clamp, wooden bar clamps have stops which can be adjusted in distance from the screw. The simplest of these is a series of holes bored equidistant from each other the length of the bar into which wooden pegs are inserted. Another device is a block fitted with a wire or strap bridle which fits into a series of notches sawn equidistant from each other of the bottom of the bar. On either type, if the stop cannot be adjusted properly, it is easy to solve the problem by boring another hole or sawing another notch.

For glueing two pieces of stuff one on top of the other, or for securing work to the top of the bench, the woodworker may use the C clamp, still commonly available in the 1970s, or the two-bar clamp, available but not common in the Industrial Age.

The C clamp is merely an iron bar bent into the shape of a C with an iron turnscrew through one of its extremities. Work is placed between the extremities and clamped by tightening the screw.

Two-bar clamps consist of two boards, usually about two inches square and fifteen inches long, each with two holes about four inches from the ends, one of them threaded. Wooden screws, with handles in opposite directions, fit into these holes. Clamping is accomplished by tightening the screws simultaneously.

C clamp

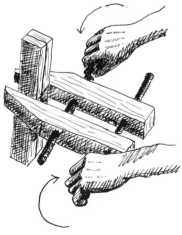

Two-bar clamp

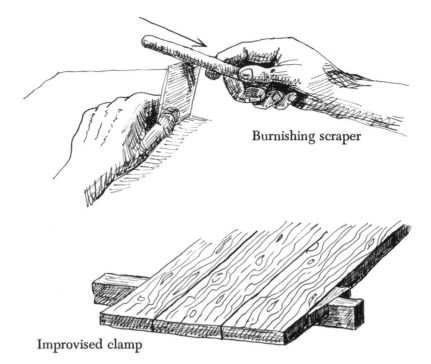

Burnishing scraper

Improvised clamp

Improvised clamps, using a wedge instead of screws, can be made with very little effort for any type of glueing, but such improvisations are not usually adjustable. For instance, bar clamps are made from a board one to two inches thick and four inches wide, by sawing into one edge to a depth of two inches and splitting out the wood between the two extreme cuts which should be at least three inches from each end. Boards being joined are laid in the opening thus formed and clamped together by tapping in a wedge between the edge of one board and the offset at one end of the clamp. A similar clamp to substitute for the two-bar clamp can be made exactly the same way from shorter but perhaps heavier pieces of scrap lumber.

There is one additional clamp found in a few old woodworking shops which was not used for glueing but for shaping the elongated handles of various chisels, hammers and of tools. It is called a handle clamp.

In appearance, the handle clamp resembles a miniature lathe, having a bed of some eight to twelve inches long with an upright post, four to six inches tall, dovetailed or mortised into each end. A wooden screw, with a sharpened metal point protruding from its tip, pierces each of the posts.

In use, the handle clamp is secured in the vise and the stuff of the handle to be formed is clamped between the two screws, metal points being placed in the centers of the ends. Handles can now be shaped with drawknife and spokeshave, the stuff being turned by hand as the shaping proceeds.

In the early nineteenth century screw-cutting lathes, developed in eighteenth century France, were available for cutting wooden screws for vises, clamps, spinning wheels, napkin presses and a host of other items, mundane and esthetic. Before 1800, however, and by many craftsmen until about 1875, screws and the threaded holes which received them were made by hand, using taps and dies identical in principle to the metal cutting taps and dies used by ironworkers.

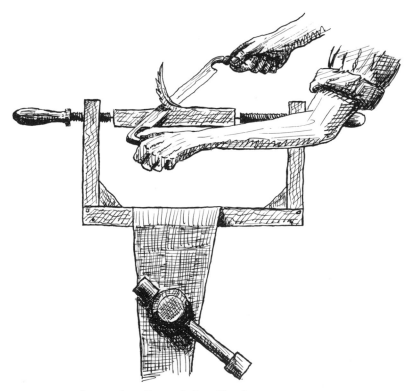

Making a handle with handle clamp

Taps are made in two forms. One, made of steel, superficially resembles an auger since its tapered square body has pointed cutting teeth filed into the corners in a spiral pattern, and its shank is inserted into an auger handle. The hole to be threaded must, of course, be of the same diameter as the diagonal dimensions of the tap at the base of the cutting teeth. It is used by inserting the tap in the hole and turning until threads are cut on the inside of the hole. Old metal taps are usual for threading small holes no more than three-quarters of an inch in diameter; modern ones, made in Europe, may be used for larger holes.

For larger holes a wooden tap with a steel cutter is employed. Its body is merely a cylindrical post from one to nine inches in diameter and from one to three feet long with a cross handle in its upper end and a saw cut spiraling up it to a point where a steel cutter is inserted through its body and secured with a small wedge. The post is inserted in an open frame which has a hole to receive it in its upper cross piece and a hole in the lower cross piece in which a small metal plate is secured. To use, this frame is secured in a vise. The wood with the hole to be threaded is placed on the lower cross piece and the dowel is inserted through the previously bored hole in the wood and down to the lower cross piece of the frame. Here the iron plate is engaged in the spiral saw cut and the dowel turned by

Metal tap

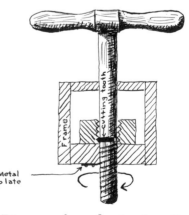

Diagram of wooden tap in action

its handle, being cammed downward all the while by the iron plate until the cutter forms the threads on the inside of the hole.

Taps of this sort are easily made by wrapping a narrow strip of paper around the dowel, marking the spiral with scriber or pencil and cutting the spiral with a saw. A tapered square hole is chiseled through the upper end to receive the cutter and wedge. Frames should be dovetailed or mortised together. Both frame and dowel should be close-grained hardwood, preferably beech.

Dies, or screw boxes, are made from two identically sized pieces of hardwood, each at least an inch thick. One has a hole bored through it of the same diameter as the diagonal dimension of the tap at the base of its cutting tooth. The other piece is bored with a hole the size of the tap at the point of its cutting tooth. The block with the smaller hole is then threaded.

Once threading is completed a slot is cut into the threaded

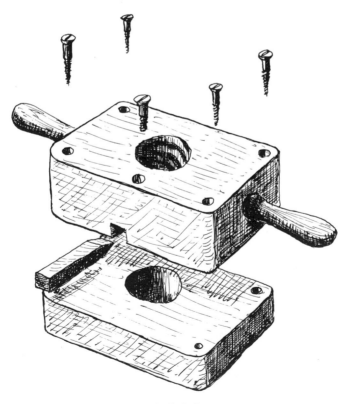

Exploded die, cutaway

block for inserting the cutter at a point where the edge of the cutter coincides with the top surface of the thread as the thread runs out. Then the other block, with the larger hole, is super-imposed on the first and the two are secured to each other with wood screws while the cutter is secured in place with either a wedge or a wood screw.

For threading large dowels it is usually necessary to have two or three screw boxes to make a series of cuts, each deeper than the last, until the threading is completed. In like manner, threading the inside of a large hole may require that the depth of the cutting tooth be adjusted so that the inside thread can be completed in two or three cuts.

In threading dowels, the work is secured in the vise so that its end may be put in the larger, unthreaded portion of the die cavity to a point where the cutting tooth prevents its further insertion. Then the screw box is turned, pressing it downward on the work, until enough thread is cut to engage in the threaded portion of the screw box. When this occurs the box may be turned with no pressure until threading is completed.

Woodcarving, an important aspect of cabinetmaking since ancient times, is more an art than a craft. It is still an active art in the latter half of the twentieth century, still requiring hand work exclusively and exactly the same tools used by the medieval carver. Because there are so many books of the tech-niques of woodcarving in existence, the art will be touched on only lightly in this book.

The tools of the woodcarver match the chisels of the turner in variety and function, the only difference being in the size. Woodcarving tools fit snugly into the palm of one hand for maximum control by the wrist. They consist of paring chisels, skew chisels, pointers, gouges, gooseneck paring chisel and gouges and innumerable other forms designed for special uses by individual carvers over the ages.

Many master carvers in the old days, and still in Europe, spurned tools designed by others and in later years would pay no attention to tools made in factories, regardless of the repu-tation of the manufacturer. Usually they designed their own tools and carefully supervised the forging and tempering by a reliable blacksmith. Frequently they would make their own with

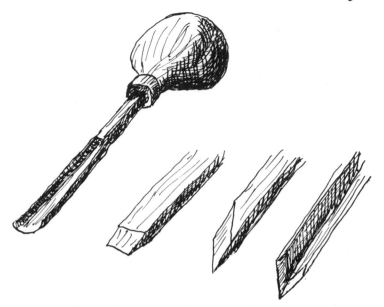

Types of wood carving tools—gouge, flat, skew, pointer

a small forge and a small anvil set in the corner of the shop, tempering with great delicacy, usually to straw or purple color as with a razor, harder than the carpenter's chisels, so that a fine edge could be maintained without wire edges, and carvings would result with a surface smooth as glass. Good tools yield such a surface and sanding carvings made with good tools is quite a superfluous activity.

Even in modern times master carvers, like the master turners of old, make their own handles, either round with a flat side or sausage shaped, or tapered and octagonal, to fit perfectly into their palm alone. As with the mundane hammer, the handles of carving tools impart accuracy and the finer nuances of the art.

There are three types of gauges used by woodworkers, two of them by both carpenters and cabinetmakers and one by the cabinetmaker alone, especially when he works with veneers.

The marking gauge is no more than a convenient scriber consisting of a stick about a half inch square and six inches long with a small steel nail piercing the center of the stick half an inch from one end. This stick is inserted through a flat piece of wood half an inch thick and two inches square which has a wooden thumb screw to secure it at any desired point on the stick. Later marking gauges, which were produced until about World War I and revived by a few tool makers in the 1970s, usually have a scale imprinted on one side starting from the point of the scriber.

Marking gauges make it quite simple to mark a long board quickly for ripping. First the square block, through which the stick is inserted, is placed so that its edge nearest the scriber point is precisely the distance to be marked, where it is secured by tightening the screw. The block acts as a fence which is placed on the edge of the board being marked while the gauge is drawn down the length of the board being slightly canted toward the worker and with slight downward pressure, the face of the fence being held tightly against the edge of the board. The result is a mechanically perfect line which coincides with the edge of the board.

Mortise gauges differ from the regular marking gauge by having two sticks inserted through the fence, each with its separate scriber. These may be adjusted so that the scriber points are divided by the width of the intended mortise, then the fence is secured to place the scriber points the correct distance from the edge of the stuff. Marking is then accomplished as with the marking gauge and repeated to duplicate the mortise width and position as many times as desired.

Cutting gauges have a small chisel-pointed knife, which protrudes about half an inch, substituted for the scriber point. Since the knife must be sharpened it is not permanently secured in the stick but is held in place by a small wedge. The cutting gauge is used mainly to cut strips of veneer accurately.

As with most wooden tools, fenced gauges might need lubrication with wax or soap or linseed oil during periods of high humidity.

Carpenters in the days of hand craftsmen usually had to transport an impressive collection of tools to the work site. Journeymen cabinetmakers, while they worked for long periods at the same bench, also had to take an even more numerous set of delicate tools from master to master. Both craftsmen required some means of carrying professional paraphernalia.

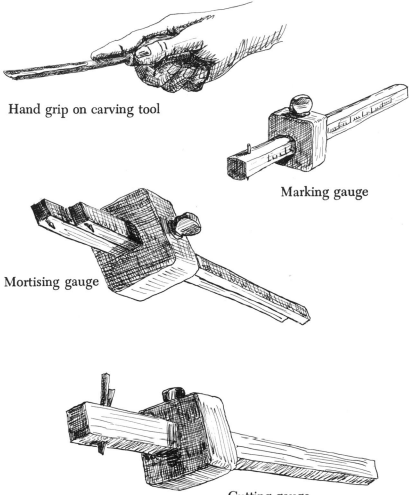

Hand grip on carving tool

Marking gauge

Mortising gauge

Cutting gauge

The carpenter's tool box often was knocked together at the work site from scrap boards and was no more than a shallow trough into which his tools were thrown helter skelter, with either a handle or a shoulder strap fastened to it.

Most traveling chests of the journeyman cabinetmaker, however, were works of art, carefully conceived and superbly joined, reflecting the generally greater artistic bent of the cabinetmaker. His chest would be made of good solid oak or beech or birch, dovetailed at the corners, its inside divided into compartments which precisely fit his planes and saws and chisels, protecting them against the jolts of coaches and wagons and the rough handling of ships' crews: an altogether more elegant container usually than his personal luggage.

The traveling problems of the journeyman were somewhat lessened in the case of traveling cabinetmakers who served the vast distances of the Southern plantation country. These itinerant craftsmen traveled in wagons loaded with choice pieces of walnut or mahogany or maple, with tool chests built into the conveyance itself. Usually they stayed at a plantation for several weeks filling orders for all sorts of furniture. If a turning was needed they would quickly construct a pole lathe, and they would use the plantation woodworking shop or construct a stout but temporary workbench beneath a protective tree for the finer nuances of planing and sawing.

Most of the articles made of wood, in old times as well as in modern days, are protected from moisture with one sort of finish or another. No paint or varnish or coat of wax can be any better than the surface it covers. Surfaces then, especially of fine furniture, must be scraped or sanded. Scrapers for flat surfaces are usually a thin piece of tempered steel with a slightly basiled edge which is burnished by drawing a hardened steel bar over the edge to turn it. Once the edge is properly prepared

Carpenter's tool chests with handle and strap

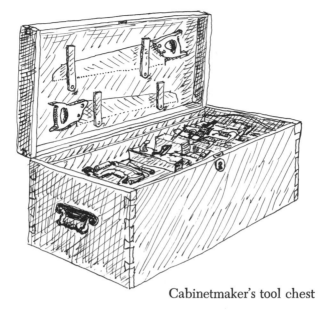

Cabinetmaker's tool chest

the scraper is held at about a 45° angle to the surface and pulled toward the worker. When the edge becomes dulled it is burnished once more.

On less elegant furniture the surface may be sanded. Before the development of factory-made sandpaper about 1860 the cabinetmaker's apprentices were usually given the job of sanding, using a barely damp piece of soft leather and a handful of fine, clean sand. The sand may be sprinkled lightly on the surface and rubbed vigorously with the leather spread out and moved with both hands. Sand adheres to damp leather for sanding vertical and oblique surfaces.

Pumice stone and soft bricks may also be used to rub a surface to perfection, preparing it for varnish, shellac or linseed oil.

Linseed oil, which comes from the seeds which grow into flax, has been a favorite and durable furniture finish since the seventeenth century at least. It must be refined by boiling before use, but its application is simple if dull. The oil is spread thinly over the surface of the wood and rubbed in with a rag for the first coat. After that it is rubbed in by the palm of the hand, the friction of flesh moving against wood generating enough heat to bake the coating of oil into an eventually deep transparent coating that emphasizes the grain and color of the natural wood. Boiled linseed oil may be applied one coat at a time for years until it forms a thick, almost mirror like, surface which embellishes the beauty of the wood.

Both lacquer and shellac were brought from the Orient by French and English and Portuguese merchants. Both have been widely used since India was first settled by Europeans in the eighteenth century, and both are still quality finishes for fine furniture. Varnish, though developed at a later date, is also popular and effective.

Common work of pine and other less valuable woods and buildings may be protected with paint. In past times paint was usually made from a base of boiled linseed oil or white lead. To this was added ocher or copper oxide, or lampblack or other ingredients which give the paint its color.

The origin of the typical American red barn, however, is based on the frugality of New England farmers who hated to waste excess milk. They mixed the cheapest of coloring ingredients, red ocher, with milk and painted their barns with the result. Milk, or course makes a fine base for paint since it includes the same adhesive substance which forms the base of modern white glues.

There are many, many types of woodworkers and many woodworking tools which remain to be described in other volumes, but the tools and techniques of the major woodworking specialists, carpenters, cabinetmakers, turners, loggers, boardmakers and adzmen provide some insight into the importance of woodworking in our history, and the skill developed by woodworkers. These skills, and the attitudes of patience, attentive care and inspiration which developed the skills, need not be lost regardless of the overwhelming dominance of the machine over late twentieth-century society.

The machine has created, and continues to create, leisure and education and artistic understanding. This leisure might be well used to revive the tools and attitudes of the hand woodworker and spawn a new era of satisfaction in individual artistic achievement. If this happens, civilization may well grow stronger from the benefits.

Bibliography

Benjamin, Asher. *The American Builder's Companion.* 1827. Reprint. New York: Dover Publications, Inc., 1969.

The Cabinetmaker in Eighteenth Century Williamsburg. Williamsburg Craft Series. Williamsburg, Virginia: 1963.

Chippendale, Thomas. *The Gentleman & Cabinetmaker's Director.* Reprint. New York: Dover Publications, Inc., 1966.

Early American Industries Association. *Chronicle.* Williamsburg, Virginia: 1933t.

Gillespie, Charles Coulston, ed. *A Diderot Pictorial Encyclopedia of Trades and Industry.* New York: Dover Publications, Inc., 1959.

Goodman, W. L. *The History of Woodworking Tools.* London: G. Bell and Sons, Ltd., 1964.

Hampton, C. W., and Clifford, E. *Planecraft.* Sheffield, England: C. and J. Hampton Ltd., 1959.

Hayward, Charles H. *Cabinet Making for Beginners.* London: Evans Brothers Ltd., 1967.

Jenkins, J. Geraint. *Traditional Country Craftsmen.* New York, Washington: Frederick A. Praeger, 1966.

Katz, Laszlo. *The Art of Woodworking and Furniture Appreciation.* New York: P.F.C. Woodworking, Inc., 1971.

Kephart, Horace, *Camping and Woodcraft.* New York: The Macmillan Company, 1945.

La Fever, Minard. *The Modern Builder's Guide.* Reprint. New York: Dover Publications, Inc., 1969.

Mercer, Henry C. *Ancient Carpenter's Tools.* Doylestown, Pennsylvania: The Bucks County Historical Society, 1951.

Moxon, Joseph. *Mechanick Exercises.* Third ed. London: 1703.

Nutting, Wallace. *Furniture Treasury.* New York: The Macmillan Company, 1924.

Peterson, Charles E., ed. *The Rules of Work of the Carpenters Company of the City and County of Philadelphia, 1786.* Princeton: The Pyne Press, 1971.

Sloane, Eric. *A Museum of Early American Tools.* New York: Wilfrid Funk, Inc., 1964.

Sloane, Eric. *A Reverence for Wood.* New York: Wilfrid Funk, Inc., 1965.

Sloane, Eric. *An Age of Barns.* New York: Funk and Wagnalls, 1967.

Spon's Mechanics Own Book. London: E. and F. N. Spon, Ltd., 1904.

Viires, A. *Woodworking in Estonia.* Published pursuant to an agreement with the Smithsonian Institution, U.S.A. and The National Science Foundation, Washington, D.C. Translated from Estonian. Jerusalem: Israel Program for Scientific Translations, 1969. (Available from the U.S. Department of Commerce, Clearinghouse for Federal Scientific and Technical Information, Springfield, Virginia, 22151.)

Welsh, Peter S. "Woodworking Tools 1600–1900." Paper 51 in *Contributions From the Museum of History and Technology,* (U.S. National Museum Bulletin 241). Washington: Smithsonian Institution, 1965.

Wigginton, Eliot, ed. *The Foxfire Book.* Garden City, New York: Doubleday and Company, Inc., 1972.

Wildurg, Frank. *Woodworking Tools at Shelburne Museum.* No. 3 in Museum Pamphlet Series. Shelburne, Vermont: The Shelburne Museum, 1947.

Williams, H. Lionel. *Country Furniture of Early America.* New York: A. S. Barnes; London: Thomas Yoseloff, Ltd., 1963.

Index